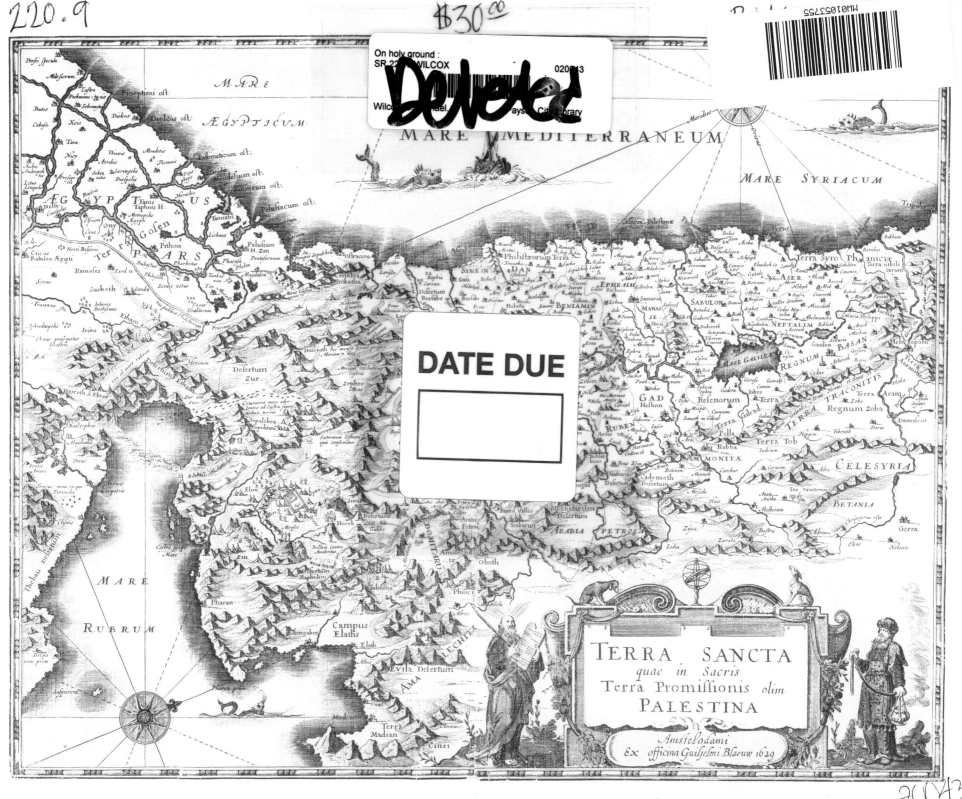

DATE DUE

TERRA SANCTA
quae in Sacris
Terra Promissionis olim
PALESTINA

Amstelodami
Ex officina Guilielmi Blaeuw 1629

On Holy Ground

On Holy Ground

IMAGES OF
OLD TESTAMENT LANDS

WRITTEN BY S. MICHAEL WILCOX

PHOTOGRAPHY BY

JOHN TELFORD • FLOYD HOLDMAN • DON THORPE • OTHERS

Covenant Communications, Inc.

Published by Covenant Communications, Inc., American Fork, Utah
Book and jacket design by Jessica A. Warner
Cover and book design © 2001 by Covenant Communications, Inc.
Copyright © 2001 Text Michael Wilcox, Photographs as per photo credit list.

Printed in Singapore.
First Printing: October 2001

08 07 06 05 04 03 02 01   10 9 8 7 6 5 4 3 2 1

ISBN 1-57734-940-7

Library of Congress Cataloging-in-Publication Data

Wlcox, S. Michael.
    On holy ground / text by S. Michael Wilcox; featuring the photography of Floyd Holdman . . . [et al.].
      p.   cm.
   ISBN 1-57734-940-7
   1. Palestine--Description and travel. 2. Israel--Description and travel. 3. Palestine in the Bible. 4. Wilcox, S. Michael--Journeys--Israel. 5. Bible. O.T.--Meditations. 6. Palestine--Pictorial works. 7. Israel--Pictorial works. I. Holdman, Floyd. II. Title.
   DS104.3 .W55 2001
   220.9'1--dc21
                2001042116

TABLE OF CONTENTS

SONG OF THE SCRIPTURES

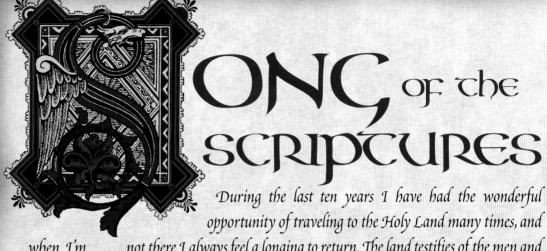

During the last ten years I have had the wonderful opportunity of traveling to the Holy Land many times, and when I'm not there I always feel a longing to return. The land testifies of the men and women whose lives are recorded in sacred writings, and above all it bears witness of the God those men and women worshiped. Their faith in Him created a dignity of character that makes them worthy of mankind's reverence and reflection.

The Old Testament is a hymn of love and praise. The different stories are the words of that song, but the melody that holds the words and gives them meaning is the love of God for His children. The personalities and events change from book to book and chapter to chapter, but the familiar music that lingers in our minds constantly reminds us of mercy, patience, forgiveness, wisdom, and compassion. It is the music of hope sung by the voices of kings and prophets, shepherd boys and little maids, widows and soldiers who knew the great Composer and understood His heart.

As I walk this chosen land, and read again the stories I knew and loved even as a boy, I hear the music and know I am part of it—we are all part of it.

A grove at Beersheba at sunset.

Inset: Woman and child in a field outside Bethlehem.

CREATION

When I first prepared to go to the Holy Land I did not think it would be a beautiful place. I pictured it as brown, barren and dusty—a harsh landscape needed to create the firmness of soul necessary for prophets and holy men. I saw it in a different light that first evening as I walked shoeless along the Mediterranean, watching the moon over the sea. A few sea birds accompanied me. They too knew the soft resistance of wet sand on bare feet. We both poked in the surf—they looking for dinner, I for colored shells. I was cooled by the sea breezes sweeping in from the west and could hear the waves pushing against the sand. The familiar passages of the opening chapter of Genesis ran through my mind with the repeated words, "and God saw that it was good." Sea and land, moonlight and cool breezes, colored shells and the feel of wet sand on bare feet, the chatter of sea birds, the taste of the salt air—it was good.

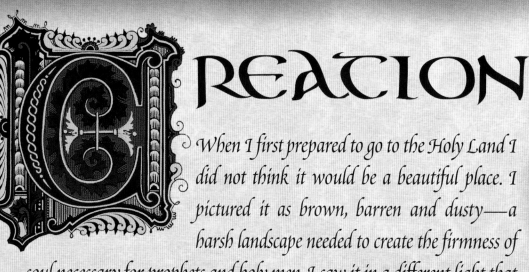

The moon over the Mediterranean Sea.

Inset: Footprint in the sand

I FILLED MY HAND WITH SAND and watched the individual grains sift through my fingers in hourglass fashion. "And were it possible that man could number the particles of the earth," Enoch wrote, "yea, millions of earths like this, it would not be a beginning to the number of thy creations" (Moses 7:30). With the words, "In the beginning," God introduced the creation we know, and yet every particle of this wonderful earth did not constitute a beginning to all God's worlds.

Rightly delighted with His creative genius, the Lord said to Moses, "Look, and I will show thee the workmanship of mine hands, but not all, for my works are without end" (Moses 1:4). It is marvelous to me to realize that among all those endless works, many aspects of creation were only prepared to fill us with a child's sense of wonder. Lest we miss that critical point, the Lord revealed that many things we see and hear and smell are simply there to "please the eye . . . to gladden the heart . . . and to enliven the soul" (D&C 59:18-19).

I turned to go, but as I left, the velvet roaring of the waves followed me. The scriptures tell us that God's voice is "as the sound of many waters" (Revelation 1:15). It is a powerful sound, but whether we listen to the waves, or a waterfall, or a mountain stream, our hearts are calmed and soothed by these echoes of our Father in Heaven's voice. This too is "good." Even the sounds of creation remind us of Him whose side we left. But lest the divine homesickness prove too harsh, lest the thin veil of forgetfulness thicken, He placed in this mortal classroom of creation a myriad of reminders of our heavenly home. If we look closely, we will see those divine footprints in the sands of the Mediterranean and in the numberless sands of His eternal creations.

(Opposite page) Light breaks through the clouds. "And God said, Let there be light: and there was light. And God saw the light, that it was good" (Gen. 1:3-4). (Right) Bird in a tree near Nazareth. "And God said, Let the waters bring forth abundantly the moving creature that hath life, and fowl that may fly above the earth in the open firmament of heaven" (Gen. 1:20).

(Below) Lilies. "And God saw every thing that he had made, and, behold, it was very good" (Gen. 1:31).

"Look and I will show thee the workmanship of mine hands"

Rainbow

When I was a boy, I learned that the rainbow was a sign that God would never again flood the earth; but modern revelation teaches us it means much more. When Enoch was shown in vision the floods swallowing up the wicked, he wept bitterly, saying, "I will refuse to be comforted" (Moses 7:44). He pleaded with the Lord to have mercy on the seed of Noah, and the Lord responded to his entreaties. "He covenanted with Enoch...that he would call upon the children of Noah" (Moses 7:51). When Noah descended from the ark, the Lord chose the rainbow as a token of His covenant with Enoch. "And the bow shall be in the cloud; and I will look upon it, that I may remember the everlasting covenant, which I made unto thy father Enoch" (Genesis 9:21, JST). That covenant included the assurance that "Zion should again come on the earth ... And the general assembly of the church of the first=born shall come down out of heaven, and possess the earth, and shall have place until the end come" (Genesis 9:21, 23 JST).

The Covenant of the Rainbow.   *Inset: Shore of the Dead Sea.*

FTER THE DARKNESS OF APOSTASY or the destruction of wickedness, a loving God sends His light bending back to the earth. He will always call upon His children until the day their righteousness becomes an invitation for Enoch's city to return. "They shall see us," the Lord told Enoch, "and we will fall upon their necks, and they shall fall upon our necks, and we will kiss each other" (Moses 7:63).

I think of these promises when I see the light of heaven split into all its glorious fullness of color. The Lord will not abandon His children. Though darkness and storm reign for a period on the earth, eclipsing the brightness of heaven, the loving light of God's gospel yearns to return, and bends in gentle tenderness to touch a cleansed earth once again.

A loving God sends His light bending back to earth.

The Lord in His mercy lowers a stairway from heaven down to earth and invites us all to climb.

the TOWER ... OR the STAIRWAY?

Early in the Old Testament we are introduced to one of the chief follies of man—his desire to build his own means of reaching heaven. In the "land of Shinar" in Mesopotamia, the people said, "Go to, let us build us a city and a tower, whose top may reach into heaven" (Genesis 11:4). The early towers of men were called ziggurats, and their terraced slopes looked like steps climbing upward. This first tower was called Babel, which comes from a Hebrew word meaning "Gate of God." Theirs was a physical tower, but the scriptures and history abound in examples of men producing their own plans for reaching heaven. Do not these man-made systems also create confusion? The Tower of Babel was built from the earth upward, but the Lord in His mercy lowers a stairway from heaven down to earth and invites us all to climb.

There is only one way to heaven. Jacob was shown that way in a revelation he received at Bethel. Bethel means "house of God." "He dreamed, and behold a ladder (better translated as stairway) set up on the earth, and the top of it reached to heaven; . . . And, behold, the Lord stood above it" (Genesis 28:12-13). When he awoke he said: "This is none other but the house of God, and this is the gate of heaven" (Genesis 28:17). Where today can we find the gate of heaven? Where is the true stairway that leads upward to a waiting Father? Is it not in the modern Bethels of the Church, the houses of God, the Holy Temples?

PATRIARCHS

I never finish reading Genesis without a renewed understanding of the power of family. From Adam's first momentous decision of choosing Eve over Eden, the person over the paradise, to Joseph's reassuring words to his brothers that he truly had forgiven them, Genesis is essentially the story of families. Surely it is no coincidence that the first book of scripture, dealing as it does with the creation of the world, begins with the early history of families.

As I retrace the footsteps of the patriarchs, the simple family messages of their lives become real and deeply applicable to my own. I am taught by my earliest parents as I hear them whisper from the places they lived: "A worthy companion is worth every effort to obtain! Counsel together when problems arise. Children are a blessing from heaven—desire them. When someone hurts you, forgive them, especially members of the family."

Arab children playing.

Inset: Jewish boy near the Western Wall.

(Top right) A woman draws water from a well in Israel. Water means life in the Middle East, and wells are dug deep into the earth to ensure a supply of life-sustaining water for both man and beast. Rebekah was "very fair to look upon," and her actions also indicate she had an inner wellspring of beauty of character and spirit.

WHENEVER I SEE A WELL IN THE HOLY LAND, I think of Rebekah and Rachel. Many of these wells require descending steps to reach the water level. Almost four thousand years ago, a young woman left her house carrying a pitcher, unaware that her destiny as a chosen matriarch depended on an act of charity and service. Abraham's servant was waiting with ten camels at the well as Rebekah approached. At his master's request he had traveled hundreds of miles over dangerous territory to find this covenant wife for Isaac.

"Shew kindness unto my master Abraham," he prayed. . . . "Let it come to pass, that the damsel to whom I shall say, Let down thy pitcher . . . that I may drink; and she shall say, Drink, and I will give thy camels drink also: let the same be she that thou hast appointed for thy servant Isaac" (Genesis 24:12,14).

In an unpremeditated act of kindness, Rebekah offered to water the ten camels. The scriptures tell us "she went DOWN to the well, and filled her pitcher, and came UP" (Genesis 24:16). As I descend the steps to the water level, I wonder at the effort that was involved as she filled her pitcher and climbed the steps over and over again to quench the thirst of ten travel-worn camels.

When the servant later asked if she would accompany him and be Isaac's wife, her simple words, "I will go," echo Nephi's own. The servant's effort to find this damsel of Haran was richly rewarded.

A young woman left her house unaware that her destiny as a chosen matriarch depended on an act of charity.

(Right) Camel caravan silhouetted against the sky in Egypt. Josephus stated that the servant commended Rebekah for her generosity and kindness in light of the fact that "it cost her some pains to draw it" (Antiquities of the Jews XVI:2). One camel can drink 20-30 gallons of water! Rebekah later rides these same camels on her journey to meet her husband. "And Rebekah arose, and her damsels, and they rode upon the camels" (Gen. 24:61).

O N THE WAY TO BETHLEHEM, we stop to visit Rachel's Tomb. Jacob was sent on the same long journey to Haran by his mother, Rebekah, to find *his* eternal companion. At the well, he would first see Rachel. "What shall thy wages be?" Laban asked him. "I will serve thee seven years for Rachel thy younger daughter" (Genesis 29:15,18). As I watch the local shepherds tending their sheep, I wonder how Rachel felt as day after day, year following year, she w a t c h e d Jacob working with her father's flocks and knew that every effort he expended was to share her companionship. She was a seven-year wife. Was Jacob satisfied with his labor? The scriptures answer, "They seemed but a few days, for the love he had to her" (Genesis 29:20).

I will serve thee seven years for Rachel, thy younger daughter.

(Opposite page) Shepherds watch their flocks today in much the same manner as they would have in Old Testament times. The quiet, pastoral life of the shepherd gave time for reflection and pondering—a natural setting for communication with the Lord. While Jacob watched his flocks, pondering Laban's change of attitude toward him, the Lord instructed him to return to his homeland. In this same setting he called his two wives to him, revealed to them his reflections and the Lord's direction, and asked for their thoughts and counsel. "And Jacob sent and called Rachel and Leah to the field unto his flock . . ." (Gen. 31:4).

(Below) This tree depicts the lineage of Jacob. Jacob felt his family was the greatest blessing he had obtained in Haran. As we read in Genesis 32, it was a concern for his wives and children that caused Jacob to "wrestle" all night with an angel, wherein his name was changed from Jacob to Israel. (According to the footnote to Genesis 32:28, this name suggests persevering or prevailing with God).

All of us are tied into this lineage as well. When we receive a patriarchal blessing, we become linked to this family. The title "patriarchal" does not refer only to the modern patriarch who pronounces the blessing upon our heads, but also refers to the great patriarchs: Abraham, Isaac, and Jacob. We receive the same promises they received, that we may have seed as numberless as the sands of the seashore or the stars of heaven if we will live righteously, following their example of obedience to eternal laws. (See D&C 132:28-33.) As the verses indicate, this promise has ramifications "out of the world."

his Tree shews that when Jacob arrived in gypt his whole family, including Joseph & is two children amounted to 70 persons. acob himself, and sixty four sons and grandsons, ne daughter Dinah, and one granddaughter Sarah, hese 37 persons, added to Joseph and his two sons ho were already in Egypt, make up the numbers xactly 70.

JACOB
Genesis. XXX. XLVI.

The two sons of Judah, Er, and Onan, who died in Canaan. Jacob's wives, their handmaidens, and his son's wives, or other connections are not taken into the number 70, here Gen. XLVI. but in Acts VII. 14.

the PEOPLE of the OLD TESTAMENT

Their family relations were tender and filled with love.

The people of the Old Testament were not a hard, unemotional people. Their family relations were tender and filled with love. When thinking of his wife, the writer of the Song of Solomon expressed the eternal nature of marital love with poetic beauty. "Set me as a seal upon thine heart, . . . for love is strong as death; . . . . Many waters cannot quench love, neither can the floods drown it . . . a man would give all the substance of his house for love . . ." (Song 8:6-7).

The Lord used the expressions of love of the husband for his wife to describe His Church in the latter days. He is the bridegroom, and we are His bride. How does He see His people? "Who is she that looketh forth as the morning, fair as the moon, clear as the sun . . ." Three times this description is applied to the Saints of the latter day. (Song 6:10; D&C 5:14; 105:31; 109:73).

(Above) A bedouin woman displays her beautifully woven tent cloth. These people show the greatest deference for visitors. From the door of a tent like this, Sarah listened to the three visitors promise her that the longed-for son would become the first of a posterity as numerous as the stars of heaven or the sands of the seashore. The woman in this photograph would be one of those descendants mentioned.

(Inset above) Black, goat-hair tent of a bedouin. Isaiah used the tent of the Middle East to describe the growth of the Church in the latter days. "Enlarge the place of thy tent, and let them stretch forth the curtains of thine habitation: spare not, lengthen thy cords, and strengthen thy stakes" (Isaiah 54:2). From this verse, we use the word "stakes" for our modern Church organizations.

ALMOST EVERYWHERE YOU GO in the Middle East, you see the black, goat-hair tents of the Bedouins. Their lives today differ very little from that of the patriarchs. I have many memories of men and women sitting together at the door of their tent or walking in the fields discussing the day-to-day problems. Without too much imagination, I can take myself back and see Abraham and Sarah, Isaac and Rebekah, Jacob, Leah, and Rachel counseling each other. The most important decisions of Genesis were always made jointly. These patriarchs listened to the wisdom of their wives, sharing with them their worries and hopes. "Separate Isaac and Ishmael," Sarah counseled. "Send Jacob to Haran for a wife," Rebekah urged. Your father's "countenance . . . is not toward me as before,"(Genesis 31:5) Jacob explained to Leah and Rachel. Was not even the decision to leave the Garden of Eden made after Adam received Eve's understanding?

Give me children, or else I die!

I F THERE IS ONE CONSISTENT THREAD that flows through Genesis, and indeed through the entire Old Testament, it is the desire for, and the joy of, children. "Look now toward heaven, and tell the stars, if thou be able to number them:" the Lord told Abraham. "So shall thy seed be" (Gen.15:5). Abraham and Sarah's reward for their faithfulness was posterity. When the promised child finally came to Sarah, she named him Isaac, which means "rejoice" or "laughter," saying, "God hath made me to laugh, so that all that hear will laugh with me" (Genesis 21:6).

"Intreat the Lord for me," Rebekah pleaded with Isaac. "And Isaac intreated the Lord for his wife, because she was barren . . . and Rebekah . . . conceived" (Genesis 25:21). "Give me children, or else I die!" Rachel cried to Jacob (Genesis 30:1). "God hath endued me with a good dowry," Leah exclaimed when her sixth son was born (Gen.esis 30:20).

The Jewish and Arab children of the Middle East are beautiful and constitute the hope of a war-weary land. Just as Isaac and Ishmael, and Jacob and Esau learned to live in peace, so too will the millenniums-old conflicts among Abraham's descendants cease. "The wolf also shall dwell with the lamb, . . . and a little child shall lead them. . . . their young ones shall lie down together. . . . They shall not hurt nor destroy in all my holy mountain" (Isaiah 11:6, 7, 9).

(Right) Hieroglyphics from the Temple of Karnak in Luxor, Egypt. (Below) Temple of Luxor at night. (Opposite page) Pillars at the Temple of Luxor. Egypt was the seedbed for the growth of the House of Israel. Its fertile soil produced the grain that fed the ancient world even through the Roman times. Perhaps it is fitting that this land of fertility, and the greatest monuments the world has known, would produce a monumental lineage of devoted righteousness; one that would feed the world spiritual bread richer than that produced on the flood plains of the Nile. Even Abraham was told that his descendants would "come out [of Egypt] with great substance" (Gen. 15:14).

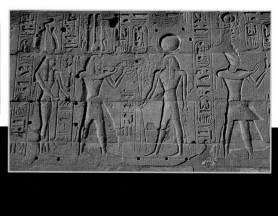

BECAUSE CHILDREN WERE SUCH A DESIRED BLESSING, the pains of past years in Joseph's life were alleviated with the birth of his two sons. As I walk through the ruins of ancient Egyptian palaces or view the treasures of pharaohs, I think of the significance of the names Joseph gave those sons. All the joys, comforts, and power of his new life could not erase the troubled memories of bondage and imprisonment until Asenath presented Joseph with children. "And Joseph called the name of the firstborn Manasseh: For God, said he, hath made me forget all my toil, and all my father's house. And the name of the second called he Ephraim: For God hath caused me to be fruitful in the land of my affliction" (Genesis. 41:51-52). Children, not power, healed his painful past.

Children, not power, healed Joseph's painful past.

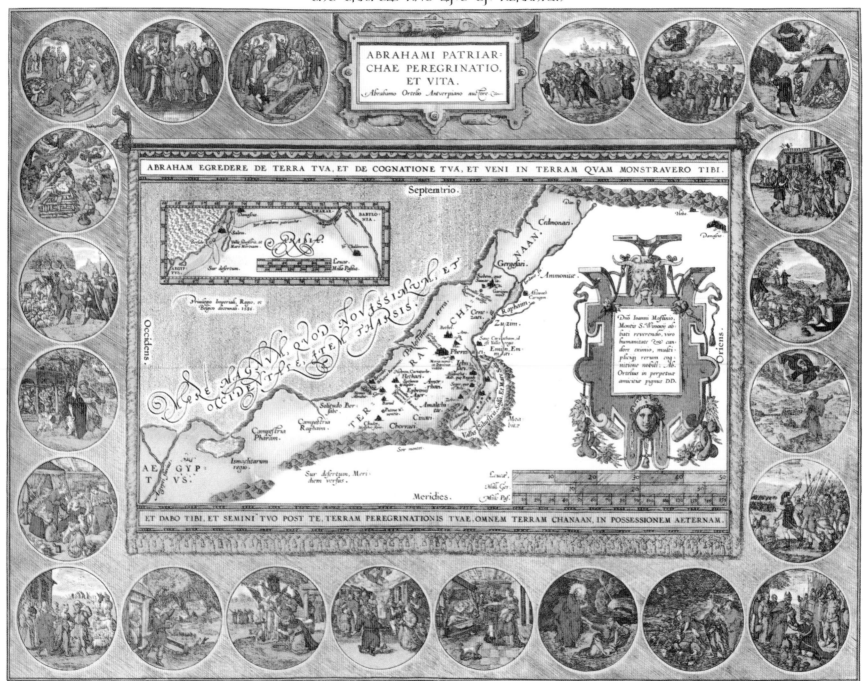

(Above) Tel Beersheba. (Right) A dove rests on barbed wire at Golgotha, symbolizing the peaceful unity foretold by Isaiah. "Blessed be Egypt my people, and Assyria (modern Iraq) the work of my hands, and Israel mine inheritance" (Isaiah 19:25).

I AM REMINDED OF THE NAMING OF ANOTHER CHILD as I sit in the ruins of Beersheba and stare out over the vast Negev wilderness. The story of that child and his mother touches me as deeply as any truth presented in Genesis. It was here that Hagar wandered with Ishmael. "And the water was spent in the bottle, and she cast the child under one of the shrubs. . . . Let me not see the death of the child. And she . . . lift up her voice, and wept" (Genesis 21:15-16). On an earlier wandering in this same area, an angel revealed to Hagar the name the Lord would have her give the unborn child she was carrying. "Behold, thou art with child, and shalt . . . call his name Ishmael; because the Lord hath heard thy affliction" (Genesis 16:11). Ishmael means "God hears." In Hagar's desperate situation, the answer lay in the name of her son. And God did hear Hagar, "And God opened her eyes, and she saw a well of water" (Genesis 21:19). This story is so sacred to the Arabs, who descend from Ishmael, that they reenact it as part of the great Mecca pilgrimage desired by every Muslim.

God loves His children and hears their cries. He is mindful of the Sarahs and Isaacs of the world, but His love is equally deep for the Hagars and the Ishmaels. I am always reminded of this story as I speak with the descendants of both Isaac and Ishmael, and watch the tragic consequences of their present conflict. A loving Father hears both of their prayers, and, perhaps, only His wisdom can bring them together in family love.

(Right) The well at Beersheba. The name Beersheba—The Well of the Oath—was given because Abraham made a covenant with the Canaanites regarding disputed water rights which ended in a peaceful settlement. However, here by the well he dug and in the shade of the "grove" he planted, his most critical trial, a trial of the soul, would begin. (Story of Abraham and the well in Genesis 21).

(Opposite page) Mt. Moriah, which is sacred to three major religions, began its long history with Abraham's sacrifice. Here, only a few hundred yards from Calvary, the Father and Son's eternal sacrifice for the salvation of mankind would be acted out in similitude. The Dome of the Rock sits over the place where, according to Islamic belief, Abraham offered Ishmael to the Lord.

FROM BEERSHEBA, my thoughts travel to Mt. Moriah in Jerusalem. It was in Beersheba that the voice of the Lord came to Abraham and said, "Take now thy son, thine only son Isaac, whom thou lovest, and get thee into the land of Moriah; and offer him there for a burnt offering" (Genesis 22:2). Two thousand years later, another Father would offer on that same mountain His only begotten and beloved Son. Perhaps the Lord wanted the first father of Israel to share, in an intimate way, an understanding of the atoning love required of both Father and Son. Though we often concentrate on the faith of Abraham, Isaac stood in the place of Christ in Genesis' great similitude. How it must have touched Abraham to see Isaac's gracious acceptance of God's command as he willingly prepared himself for the sacrifice. How it touches us to know that the pain our Father in Heaven felt for His suffering Son could be endured because of the love He held for His other children.

That sacrifice allows us to receive forgiveness, but the Savior Himself often attached a condition. "Forgive us our debts, as we forgive our debtors," Jesus taught us to pray. I ponder these words in my own life as I stand on a hill looking down the Jabbok River Valley and reflect on the meeting of two brothers, Jacob and Esau, one forgiving, and the other in need of the offered mercy.

How it must have touched Abraham to see Isaac's gracious acceptance of God's command.

A S JACOB RETURNED TO CANAAN, and heard Esau was coming to meet him with four hundred men, he feared for his life and the lives of his family. All night long he "wept, and made supplication" while he "wrestled" with the Lord "until the breaking of the day" (Hosea 12:4; Genesis 32:24). Esau's heart was full of compassion, and "Esau ran to meet him, and embraced him, and fell on his neck, and kissed him: and they wept" (Genesis 33:4). In words reminiscent of the Prodigal Son, two brothers found peace in forgiveness after twenty years of separation.

I N THE SHADOWS OF THE GREAT PYRAMIDS of Egypt I think of the beauty of family forgiveness. Joseph, judged and condemned by his brothers, was sold into thirteen years of bondage. Those same brothers, threatened by famine, bowed before him in prophetic fulfillment of his previous dreams. Somewhere in these halls of Egypt, aware of the guilt that had haunted them for the last twenty years, Joseph "could not refrain himself . . . And he wept aloud: . . . And Joseph said unto his brethren, I am Joseph . . . Come near to me, I pray you. . . . I am Joseph your brother . . . . Now therefore be not grieved, nor angry with yourselves, that ye sold me hither: for God did send me before you to preserve life. . . . So now it was not you that sent me hither, but God" (Genesis 45:1-8).

I am impressed with the majesty and towering height of the pyramids; however, the highest monument of human greatness ever constructed in Egypt was built with the tears, kindness, and forgiving embraces of a brother.

Seventeen years later, at the death of Jacob, Joseph's brothers still could not believe in the full forgiveness they had received and bowed once again before him. Weeping as he listened to them, he said, "Fear ye not: I will nourish you, and your little ones. And he comforted them, and spake kindly unto them" (Genesis 50:21). I see in Joseph a type for the Savior. How often has He told us "Thy sins are forgiven thee; go in peace," only to watch us depart still harbouring the lingering traces of painful guilt. Perhaps He weeps as did Joseph. Let us give him the victory He paid such a terrible price to win.

(Opposite page) Looking east at the Great Pyramid of Chaeops (also known as Khufu's pyramid) at Giza, Egypt. Built ca. 2575 B.C., this pyramid is 481 feet tall, and was the tallest monument in the world until the 19th century. Much of the building of pyramids took place during the months when the Nile flooded the cultivated fields so the idled farmers could be put to work on construction crews. For King Khufu's pyramid, workers prepared and set in place approximately 2.3 million stone blocks, each weighing an average of two and a half tons.

(Right) Sunset on the Nile River at Luxor, Egypt. In this fertile land abounding with plenty, Jacob prophesied that Joseph would inherit an even more blessed land. "Joseph is a fruitful bough by a well; whose branches run over the wall" (Gen. 49:22). We interpret this to mean America, a land enriched "with blessings of heaven above, blessings of the deep that lieth under" (Gen. 49:25).

(Below) In contrast, we see three camels lying in front of the Great Pyramids of Egypt—an area abundantly rich in ancient history, yet barren and untouched by the life-giving waters of the Nile River.

(Opposite page) Man and water buffalo walking on the banks of the Nile River, Egypt.

EACH TIME I LEAVE THE RUINED TEMPLES and palaces of ancient Egypt, a land of stark contrast between the life-barren, dry sands of the desert and the rich bounty of the Nile's floodplains, I reflect on the great contrasts of Joseph's life. The land itself seems to teach one of the great messages a loving Father in Heaven so wishes us to receive. God's love, like an ever-flowing river, will bring life and plentiful harvests even in the harshest conditions of mortality. In the winds that blow in from the desert, I seem to hear an ancient patriarch whisper, "Maintain a life of integrity and righteousness even in the face of tremendous injustice and temptation. Forgive with Christlike mercy and compassion; then God can, and will, turn all your sorrows to goodness and joy."

I N HEBRON, the final family truth presented in Genesis comes to me as we visit the tombs of the patriarchs. As these great men reached the culmination of their lives, their deaths are described with a phrase that is rich in meaning. "Then Abraham gave up the ghost, . . . and was gathered to his people" (Genesis 25:8). The same words are used for Isaac and Jacob. They were buried together with the women who loved them. Just before he died, Joseph "said unto his brethren, "I die, and go unto my fathers; and I go down to my grave with joy" (Genesis 50:24, JST).

The bonds of family love forged in life do not end in the grave. Our "people" wait for us on the other side; therefore, we may, as did Joseph, go to them "with joy." What wonderful reunions have been held beyond the veil. As I leave Hebron, where my ancient fathers and mothers once lay awaiting the resurrection of Christ, I realize that I too will one day be gathered to my people—including these wonderful mothers and fathers of Genesis, whose lives have inspired and taught me how to make my own family an eternal one.

(Left) Tomb of the Patriarchs in Hebron. This site, honored from ancient times, is the second most holy Jewish shrine. The present building is a mosque built over the cave Abraham bought for Sarah's burial.

up to BETHEL

Jacob dreamed of a stairway that climbed to heaven.

From the top of a small hill, I can see the ancient site of Bethel. Bethel means "House of God." This is holy ground and I sense a special spirit of reverence that has remained here since Jacob first had his dream of the stairway that climbed to heaven. When Jacob returned from Haran with his family, the Lord commanded him to bring them to Bethel. "Put away the strange gods that are among you," Jacob instructed them, "and be clean, and change your garments: And let us arise, and go up to Beth-el" (Genesis 35:2-3). I feel the heavy responsibility of fatherhood, and the need to follow Jacob's example. Has not the Lord also commanded the fathers of today to prepare their families to go up to the temples, the modern Bethels? We must teach them to put away the things of the world, and to be clean, for Bethel is a holy place where God reveals Himself to His children.

(Right) Ancient wall at Bethel. Formerly called Luz (Gen. 28:19), Bethel is one of Israel's most sacred places. Abraham built an altar here upon his arrival in Canaan; here Jacob had his dream; and it was also a place of sanctuary during Samuel's life.

Into the Wilderness

Whenever I visit the Middle East, I try to get down into the Negev or the Sinai desert. It was here that the children of Israel wandered for forty years. It is hard to imagine anything surviving the desolation spread before me. One may find an occasional oasis, but for the most part, all that greet the eye are barren stretches of sand and rock. Someday I would like to retrace on foot the wanderings of Israel as they followed Moses out of Egypt toward the Promised Land. In a very real way, their journey represents the journey of all mankind. Their journey was physical, ours spiritual; but the conditions, challenges, and blessings of the Lord are the same.

Bedouin woman walking near palm trees in Egypt.

Inset: Blossoming bushes and date palms in Egypt.

As we read Exodus and Numbers, we are invited to apply the events of their remarkable wandering years to our own journey through life. Paul explained this to the Corinthian saints when he said, "Now all these things happened unto them for ensamples: and they are written for our admonition, upon whom the ends of the world are come" (1 Corinthians 10:11). No other Old Testament story is referred to in other scripture as much as the Exodus. It is a Mosaic endowment designed to be applied in the same manner as the narrative of the temple.

In the Negev or the Sinai, one is always looking for life, for water. I have reflected on the appropriateness of this wilderness as a symbol for mortality. In a fallen telestial world, we too often search anxiously for spiritual nourishment. We look for guides who know how to survive in the mortal desert of modern morality. Who can direct us, not only to the sources of life, but also to the promised land of our eternal home?

Who can direct us to the promised land of our eternal home?

(Far left) Pharaoh's daughter was one of two women whose mission was foretold. "A seer will I raise up to deliver my people out of the land of Egypt: and he shall be called Moses. And by this name he shall know that he is of thy house; for he shall be nursed by the king's daughter, and shall be called her son" (JST Gen. 50:29). The Lord knew the heart of Pharaoh's daughter. Trusting the natural sympathies of a woman, He placed his chosen deliverer in the compassionate arms of one who could raise a baby of another race as her own.

(Left) Sinai desert. It was on Mt. Sinai that Moses received his call, as the Lord spoke to him from the burning bush. "I have surely seen the affliction of my people . . . and have heard their cry . . . for I know their sorrows; And I am come down to deliver them . . ." (Exodus 3:7-8).

(Opposite page) Map, oriented to the east, showing the Holy Land divided into the Tribes on both sides of the Jordan River, the shoreline extending from Sidon to Alexandria. Along the top and the bottom are 18 vignettes depicting the Exodus. At the bottom left is a miniature inset view of Jerusalem. The path the Children of Israel took from Egypt to the land of promise is indicated by a yellow line.

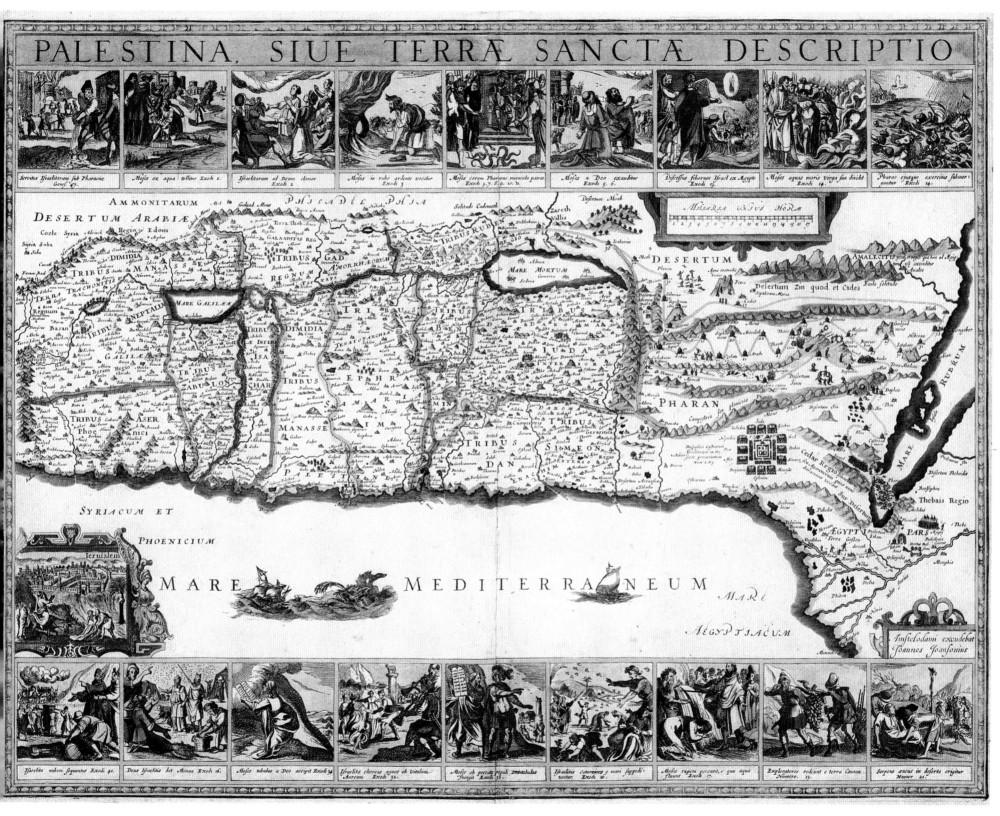

PALESTINA, SIUE TERRÆ SANCTÆ DESCRIPTIO

(Below) Moses strikes the rock in Horeb, and water springs forth.

(Right) Sands of the Sinai Desert. Moses was instructed to write a song for the Children of Israel to sing to help them remember the lessons of the wilderness. In the song, we find these words: "He [God] found him [Israel] in a desert land, and in the waste howling wilderness; he led him about, he instructed him as the apple of his eye.
As an eagle stirreth up her nest, fluttereth her wings, taketh them, beareth them on her wings; So the Lord alone did lead him . . ."
(Deut. 32:10-12).

(Opposite page) Map detailing the wanderings of the Children of Israel through the wilderness.

The fountain of living waters is representative of the love of God.

As I sit in the warm desert sand, reading of manna and of water from the rock, of burning pillars of fire, and brazen serpents, the great lessons and assurances of these stories testify to the mercy of the Lord. I hear again that same sweet music of compassion, patience, and understanding that constitutes the foundation of the Old Testament. I am encouraged in my own wilderness wanderings, knowing the Lord has foreseen the difficulties and will teach me how to endure. Moses' prayer affirms this.

"Thou in thy mercy hast led forth the people . . . thou hast guided them in thy strength unto thy holy habitation" (Exodus 15:13).

"What shall we drink?" the people asked. And the Lord answered with water from the Rock. Nephi tells us that the "fountain of living waters . . . are a representation of the love of God" (I Nephi 11:25). Christ is the Rock, and from Him flows pure love. If we are spiritually aware, we will find manifestations of this love throughout our journey. When our spirits thirst, the rock will open and life will be sustained.

"Ye have brought us forth into this wilderness, to kill this whole assembly with hunger," the people cried to Moses. "I will rain bread from heaven for you," the Lord responded (Exodus 16:3-4). Each morning the children of Israel gathered the manna that would sustain them through the day. After forty years of feasting on the Lord's bread, Moses taught them a deeper meaning to this daily miracle.

"He humbled thee, and suffered thee to hunger, and fed thee with manna . . . that he might make thee know that man doth not live by bread only, but by every word that proceedeth out of the mouth of the Lord doth man live" (Deuteronomy 8:3).

Each time I travel this wilderness, I wonder what it would have been like to see the manna cover the ground each morning. What did it taste like? Did it fully satisfy their hunger? With those questions comes the realization that I hold in my hands the bread from heaven, the nourishing words of God recorded for all to read. Like the Israelites, we must gather it "every morning" if we hope to attain the promised land. Through the great silence of the desert, it is not hard to hear the words of Moses still echoing. "In the morning, then ye shall see the glory of the Lord; . . . This is the bread which the Lord hath given you to eat" (Exodus 16:7, 15).

(Above) A crocodile fish lies partially covered on the bottom of the Red Sea.

(Above) The brightly colored butterfly fish.

(Above) A lion fish is one of the more exotic life forms in the Red Sea.

(Background) The Red Sea from the shores of Egypt. The Red Sea, located between Egypt and Arabia, was miraculously parted so the Israelites could pass through on dry land. Sharks, sea turtles, barracuda, manta rays, triggerfish, moray eels, Napoleon wrasses, and numerous brightly colored coral and fish make this underwater canvas breathtakingly beautiful and teeming with life.

The calls of worldly bondage will fade when our eyes are on the uplifted rod in our prophet's hands.

The CHILDREN OF ISRAEL were not left to wander the desert's vastness without direction. They were guided by two main sources: the firm leadership of Moses, and the ever-present pillar of fire. Jethro described the role of Moses as a prophet leader when he counseled him after the Red Sea crossing. "Be thou for the people to Godward, that thou mayest bring the causes unto God: And thou shalt teach them ordinances and laws, and shalt shew them the way wherein they must walk, and the work that they must do" (Exodus 18:19-20).

Men like Moses still lead the Lord's children. With their own personal example of righteousness, they show us the way we must walk.

But the people were reluctant to follow Moses. With every new challenge, they cried for the fleshpots and brick pits of Egypt. Even though turning back to Egypt meant contin-ued slavery, they preferred the security of bondage over freedom with faith.

Though the wilderness may be harsh, and the path the prophet asks us to travel may be difficult, we must not look back. The calls of worldly bondage will fade into the distance when our eyes are continuously fastened on the uplifted rod in our prophet's hands—the word of God—which beckons us forward.

The pillar of fire also guided the children of Israel. "And the Lord went before them by day in a pillar of a cloud, to lead them the way; and by night in a pillar of fire, to give them light; to go by day and night: He took not away the pillar . . . from before the people" (Exodus 13:21-22). When the pillar rested on the tabernacle, the people stayed in camp, but when the pillar moved, "whether it was by day or by night . . . whether it were two days, or a month, or a year" (Numbers 9:21-22), they followed the pillar.

We too are invited to follow the pillar of fire. Today that pillar burns within our hearts as we listen to the directions of the Holy Spirit. As I gaze across the desert, I realize how fearful this journey would be without the reassurance that One who knows the way is leading my footsteps. With that thought, I understand better why the Holy Ghost is called the Comforter. How comforting it must have been for our ancient ancestors to look through the open flaps of their tents in the darkness of the desert night, and see the light of God's guiding fire still hovering protectively over them.

GREATER THAN THE TREASURES OF EGYPT

King Tutenkamen's gold funeral mask. Tutenkamen reigned during the 18th Dynasty. By this time, the kings were no longer building pyramids. Possibly in an effort to foil looters, their graves were cut into desert cliffs in Luxor (Thebes). Tutenkamen's Tomb was discovered in 1922, and the treasures found there give us a glimpse of that golden era.

Time after time while traveling in the wilderness, the children of Israel longed to go back to Egypt. "We remember the fish, which we did eat in Egypt freely;" they cried, "the cucumbers, and the melons, and the leeks, and the onions, and the garlick: but now our soul is dried away: there is nothing at all, beside this manna, before our eyes" (Numbers 11:5-6). While reading these words, I cannot help but be impressed with Moses' attitude in contrast. "By faith Moses, when he was come to years, refused to be called the son of Pharaoh's daughter; Choosing rather to suffer affliction with the people of God, than to enjoy the pleasures of sin for a season; Esteeming the reproach of Christ greater riches than the treasures in Egypt . . . By faith he forsook Egypt" (Hebrews 11:24-27).

I have walked amidst the grandeur of Egyptian palaces and temples, and spent hours gazing on the wonderful treasures of the Pharaohs on display in Cairo. Often in front of Tutenkamen's golden coffins, I read of Moses's decision, and my appreciation for this great prophet deepens. In light of his sacrifice, my own temptations with worldly riches and comforts seem trivial. He sought higher treasures, and discovered the wealth of the soul.

THE LORD DID NOT LEAD THEM in a straight course from Egypt to the Promised Land. They turned south down the Sinai peninsula to a mountain where they would "meet with God" (Exodus 19:17). Here the Lord would make them "a kingdom of priests, and an holy nation" (Exodus 19:6). From the thundering heights of Mt. Sinai they heard the Lord deliver His law, and they promised obedience.

I have never been to Sinai, but I have been many times to the Lord's holy mountain: His temples—our *modern* Sinais. Here we too may meet with God and receive His laws and make covenants of obedience. Here we become a kingdom of priests and a holy nation. One cannot reach the promised land without first visiting Sinai.

But the Lord would do more than give the children of Israel laws and covenants from His holy mountain. He would not send them on their journey alone. "My presence shall go

(Right) Sunrise seen from Mt. Sinai.

(Inset right) Mountains of Sinai in early morning light. Mt. Siani is located in the southern Sinai peninsula. After the Children of Israel built the golden calf, Moses returned to the heights of Sinai to receive the commandments once again from a forgiving Lord. Though the mountain had earlier thundered and shook with revelatory power, it was now at rest in the soothing light of mercy.

temples testify to this truth just as the wilderness tabernacle did so many years ago.

Passing down the long Arabah Valley toward the Red Sea, I think of Christ and His atoning mercy. Somewhere along this route, one of the great types of His future sacrifice was shown to the people. The country is stark and hard, and it is easy to understand why "the soul of the people was much discouraged because of the way" (Numbers 21:4). Discouragement led to complaining. "There is no bread, neither is there any water; and our soul loatheth this light bread." Then came the "fiery serpents . . . and they bit the people" (Numbers 21:5-6).

Realizing their error, the children of Israel pleaded with Moses to intercede with the Lord and take away the serpents. "Make thee a fiery serpent, and set it upon a pole," the Lord instructed, "and it shall come to pass, that every one that is bitten, when he looketh upon it, shall live" (Numbers 21:8).

The fiery serpents represent the temptations which, when we give way to them, cause pain and may lead to spiritual death. But the Savior won a victory over the serpent when He atoned in Gethsemane and on Calvary. In the ancient world, a king who defeated another would often put the conquered king's head or body on a pole and lift it up. The bronze serpent was a reminder of Christ's complete victory over His adversary.

Our Savior knows we will often be bitten, especially when discouragement sets in, or we tire of eating the manna of His word in our longing for the sharper tastes of the world. There is a source of healing. We are asked to do a simple thing: look to Christ with faith, and believe in His offered forgiveness and mercy. He is tender in His feelings for us just as He was with the children of Israel. In much the same way as an indulging parent seeks to satisfy a child, so the Lord shows His kindness and care for His wandering children.

As I leave the parched Arabah, the words of the psalmist come to mind. His thoughts upon the journey of the children of Israel seem to express my own, and I realize this wonderful story has inspired the Lord's children for many centuries. "But he, being full of compassion, forgave their iniquity . . . yea, many a time turned he his anger away . . . For he remembered that they were but flesh; a wind that passeth away, and cometh not again" (Psalms 78:38-39).

The fiery serpents represent the temptations that may lead to spiritual death.

with thee, and I will give thee rest" (Exodus 33:14). The Lord made this promise even after they had violated their covenants by making and worshiping the golden calf, which caused Moses to conclude that, "The Lord God, [was] merciful and gracious, longsuffering, and abundant in goodness and truth, Keeping mercy for thousands, forgiving iniquity and transgression and sin" (Exodus 34:6-7).

The people built the Lord a tent for Him to dwell in while they traveled. This tabernacle was a constant reminder to all who saw it that the Lord dwelt with His people. When I see the lights shining on the temples, I too am reminded that the Lord still dwells with His people. Our

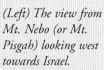

(Left) The view from Mt. Nebo (or Mt. Pisgah) looking west towards Israel.

(Below) View across the Dead Sea toward Mt. Nebo.

RELEASE FROM MT. NEBO

After decades of service, the time for Moses' release drew near. The Lord called him to the top of Mt. Nebo. From this high vantage point you can see the Dead Sea, the Judean Wilderness, the hills of Judea where Jerusalem lies, and the long Jordan River Valley stretching north. At the foot of this mountain, the camp of Israel waited in the Plains of Moab for the command to cross the Jordan into the Promised Land. Moses longed to go with them, to attain the goal he had pursued for so many years. However, another great prophet would conquer the land.

A wonderful feeling that reveals the Lord's wisdom and kindness pervades the summit of Mt. Nebo. I believe most of us can understand Moses' desires. We have had callings we loved so deeply that the release was painful. We often feel there is still so much we would like to do. The Lord was aware of Moses' emotions, and took him to a mountain top where he could see the fruits of his faithful service. He had brought them this far, and the Lord was pleased with his labors. Perhaps the warm feelings one experiences on this mountain top express the Lord's pleasure with all of our service to His kingdom. At any rate, it is a lesson to us all when various releases of life come—be it Church callings, the departure of children from our homes, or even death itself—to pause long enough to see how we have helped others progress towards their eternal home.

Choose Ye This Day

As Israel moved into the land of Canaan, they faced both a physical and a spiritual battle. Under Joshua's leadership they were to conquer the land, while refusing to be influenced by the practices and morality of the Canaanites. This second battle would prove more difficult than the first. To emphasize the need to obey the Lord rather than accept the beliefs and behaviors of those around them, the Lord commanded Joshua to bring the people to Shechem where they were told, "Choose you this day whom ye will serve" (Joshua 24:15).

Terraced hillside in Israel.   Inset: Schechem.

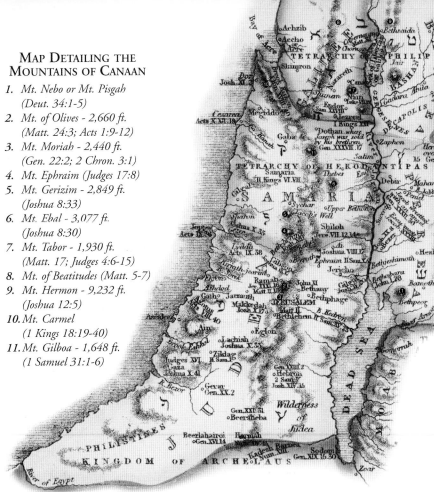

MAP DETAILING THE MOUNTAINS OF CANAAN

1. *Mt. Nebo or Mt. Pisgah
(Deut. 34:1-5)*
2. *Mt. of Olives - 2,660 ft.
(Matt. 24:3; Acts 1:9-12)*
3. *Mt. Moriah - 2,440 ft.
(Gen. 22:2; 2 Chron. 3:1)*
4. *Mt. Ephraim (Judges 17:8)*
5. *Mt. Gerizim - 2,849 ft.
(Joshua 8:33)*
6. *Mt. Ebal - 3,077 ft.
(Joshua 8:30)*
7. *Mt. Tabor - 1,930 ft.
(Matt. 17; Judges 4:6-15)*
8. *Mt. of Beatitudes (Matt. 5-7)*
9. *Mt. Hermon - 9,232 ft.
(Joshua 12:5)*
10. *Mt. Carmel
(1 Kings 18:19-40)*
11. *Mt. Gilboa - 1,648 ft.
(1 Samuel 31:1-6)*

SHECHEM LIES BETWEEN MT. EBAL AND MT. GERIZIM. These two mountains symbolized the choice the people would face every day in their new land. Following the instructions of the Lord, the twelve tribes divided into two groups. From Shechem it is not hard to imagine the tribes climbing to the peaks: six on one mountain, six on the other. The blessings for obedience and the cursings for disobedience to the Lord's commandments were read from the Law of Moses. Mt. Gerizim was the hill of blessing; Mt. Ebal was the hill of cursing.

(Right) Ruins of Shechem. The children of Israel brought Joseph's bones back from Egypt and buried them here in Shechem. See Joshua 24:32.

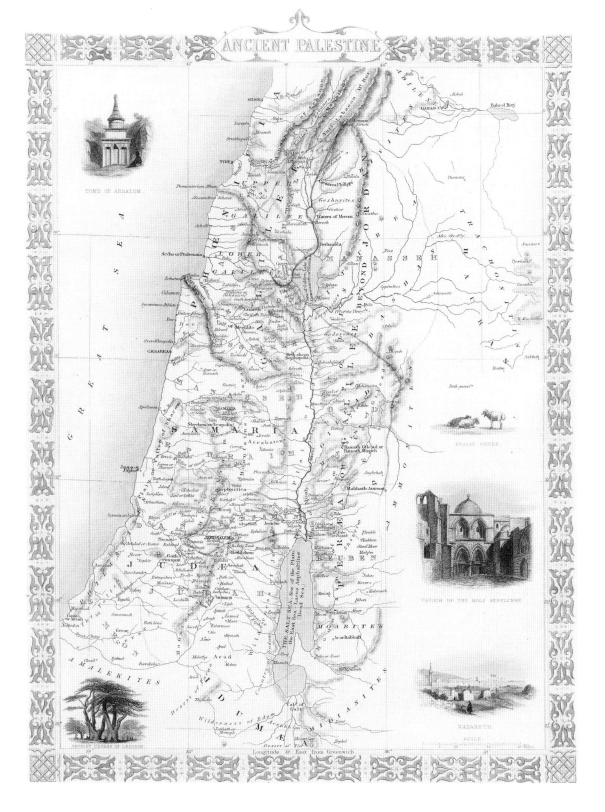

Spiritually speaking, we have all stood at the foot of these two hills. Each day of our lives we make choices. Will we receive the blessings of Gerizim through obedience, or the cursings of Ebal through disobedience? Though Jericho is a site generally associated with Joshua, it is at Shechem that I feel his influence most strongly. For it is here that he came at the conclusion of his life to deliver his final exhortation. With the two hills of choice as a backdrop, Joshua revealed the secret to a life of joy. "Choose you this day whom ye will serve . . . but as for me and my house, we will serve the Lord" (Joshua 24:15).

(Left) The divisions, cities, and towns marked on this map follow those indicated in the book of Joshua. Mt. Hor, the southern end of the Lebanon Mountains, constitutes the northern border. Beersheba, the Wilderness of Edom, and the Desert of Zin formed the southern border; and the Dead Sea, land of Moabites, Sea of Galilee, and the Jordan River constituted the eastern border. The western border was to be the Mediterranean Sea, but the Jews were not successful in expelling the Phoenicians and Philistines from the coastal area.

The only river in the Holy Land that flows continually without drying up is the Jordan. The Jordan's headwaters are at Dan and Caesarea Philippi, and the river passes through the Sea of Galilee and on to the Dead Sea. Apparently the Israelites crossed the Jordan near Bethabara (near the northern end of the Dead Sea). The southern end of the Dead Sea was formerly a fertile and populous plain on which the cities of Sodom, Gomorrha, Admah, and Zeboim once stood.

It is probable that Jerusalem, the later capital of Judah, is the Salem of which Melchizedek was king at the time of Abraham. Jerusalem ceased to be the capital of all of Israel at the revolt of the ten tribes, but was still the royal city of the southern kingdom of Judah.

CHOOSE YE THIS DAY   47

THE ISRAELITES WERE NOT THE ONLY ONES who were asked to choose. The Lord, ever rich in mercy, offered the Canaanites forgiveness, and a name and heritage among the Israelites if they would reject their false gods and immoral practices. The fall of Jericho dramatically illustrates the extended hand of Jehovah to any who were willing to grasp it. Within the city walls lived a harlot named Rahab. "The Lord your God, he is God in heaven above, and in earth beneath," she testified to the spies she hid (Joshua 2:11). She accepted Jehovah, and He rewarded her choice. She saved not only herself from destruction, but all her family as well. In time, she would marry into a noble family of Judah, become the mother of Boaz, the ancestor of David and the kings of Judah, and be mentioned by name in Christ's own genealogy.

There is not much left of Jericho for a visitor to see, so I sit at the top of its ruins, close my eyes and listen for the sound of trumpets and the tramping of feet. It is the *sound* of Jericho, not the sight, that brings the lesson home. If we listen carefully, we will hear mercy in the notes. The trumpets were blown as a warning, a final invitation to repent before the destruction began. Rahab and her family need not have been the only citizens of Jericho to live.

For seven days the Israelites marched around the city, blowing their ram's horns. On the final day, they circled Jericho seven times before they shouted in triumph as the great walls came down. An earlier generation refused to inherit the land because of their fear of Canaanite walls. How insignificant they were when finally faced. Perhaps our own walls of opposition are equally frail if we have faith.

If we listen carefully, we will hear mercy in the notes sounded as a warning.

(Left) Hebrew shofar, or ram's horn trumpet, was blown by ancient Hebrews in battle and in high religious observances. It is blown in synagogues before and during RoshHashanah.

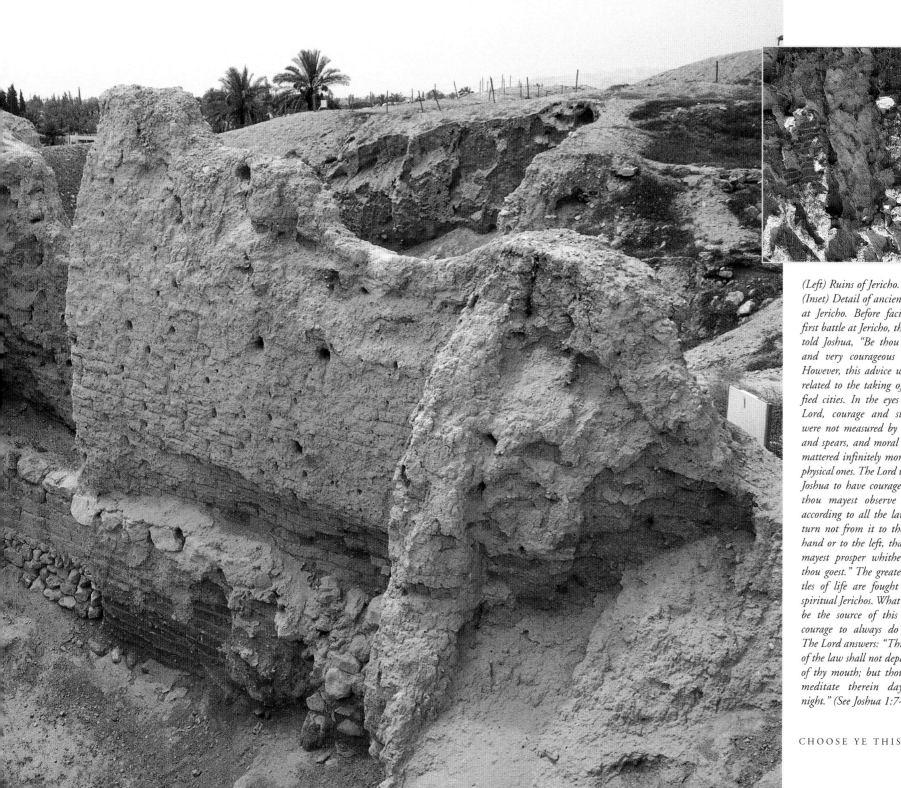

(Left) Ruins of Jericho.
(Inset) Detail of ancient walls at Jericho. Before facing his first battle at Jericho, the Lord told Joshua, "Be thou strong and very courageous . . ." However, this advice was not related to the taking of fortified cities. In the eyes of the Lord, courage and strength were not measured by swords and spears, and moral battles mattered infinitely more than physical ones. The Lord wanted Joshua to have courage, "that thou mayest observe to do according to all the law . . . turn not from it to the right hand or to the left, that thou mayest prosper whithersoever thou goest." The greatest battles of life are fought before spiritual Jerichos. What would be the source of this moral courage to always do right? The Lord answers: "This book of the law shall not depart out of thy mouth; but thou shalt meditate therein day and night." (See Joshua 1:7-8).

(Opposite) Women harvesting in a field of wheat in Israel. Gleaning was allowed by the law of Moses to provide means for the poor to care for themselves if they were willing to labor. The gleaners followed the harvesters picking up what they dropped, or gathering grain around the edges of the fields. Understanding the work involved, Boaz thoughtfully instructed his reapers to "let fall also some of the handfuls of a purpose for her, and leave them, that she may glean them, and rebuke her not" (Ruth 2:16).

LOOKING EAST FROM JERICHO, one sees the hills of Moab. In some village among these hills, Ruth was born, married an Israelite husband, and soon thereafter buried him. Near the borders of the land, probably somewhere along the Jordan River, Ruth made her choice. In words that move us still, she left her parents, her past, her people, and her gods to go with Naomi. "Intreat me not to leave thee, or to return from following after thee: for whither thou goest, I will go; and where thou lodgest, I will lodge: thy people shall be my people, and thy God my God" (Ruth 1:16).

In her poverty, Ruth gleaned in the fields of Bethlehem to care for her mother-in-law, who, in her turn, wished only the best for Ruth. "Shall I not seek rest for thee," Naomi said, "that it may be well with thee?" (Ruth 3:1). A marriage with the kindly Boaz was arranged, and from Ruth, a Moabite, would spring the Messiah of the world.

Ruth's devotion testifies that trials need not diminish our charity.

I watch the women harvesting barley in the fields around Bethlehem and think of Ruth. Her devotion testifies to us that we do not need to let the trials and hardness of life diminish our charity and compassion. Both Naomi and Ruth found strength and comfort to face sorrow in their selfless caring for each other. The Book of Ruth breathes the loving spirit of the Gospels in the New Testament. Perhaps it is not a coincidence that Bethlehem, the place of Christ's birth, was the home of these two gentle women.

(Left) Stalks of wheat in the Ayalon Valley.

Depiction of the Philistines in hieroglyphics found on the walls of the Mortuary Temple of Ramses III at Medinet Habu in Upper Egypt.

(Below) The Demise of Samson.

(Opposite) Ruins at Ashkelon. Ashkelon was one of the five Philistine cities located along the coast of Palestine from Joppa southward. Amos indicated that the Philistines came from the island of Crete (Amos 9:7). The name Palestine comes from the Greek and Roman name for "the land of the Philistines." Samson slew thirty men from Ashkelon to pay the wager he lost at his marriage. The fallen columns in the photograph remind us of how Samson was tied between the columns in Gaza. He pulled them down, ending his own life and the lives of many Philistines—a poignant lesson about binding and blinding. Samson allowed the Philistines to do both. The scriptures teach us that the adversary also desires to blind and bind us all. If we stay true to our covenants he will not be able to do so.

Was Samson the strongest man in the Bible . . . or the weakest?

DESCENDING THE HILLS OF JUDEA westward from Bethlehem brings us to the Sorek Valley in less than an hour. In the time of the Judges, this was a no-man's-land between the hills of Israel and the coastal plains of the Philistines. It was up and down this valley where Samson roamed—caught between the attractions of two vastly different worlds.

Samson was born a Nazarite from his mother's womb. Nazarites took extra vows of separation. They were dedicated to the service of the Lord, and the outward sign of their covenants was the length of their hair. Though he would win all his physical battles with the Philistines, Samson would lose the spiritual one.

The geography of Sorek seems to represent the personal war that raged within Samson all his life. Standing in the middle of the valley and looking east, I can see the highlands where Israel dwelt. It was a land of covenants which, if obeyed, would keep the Lord's people safe from the temptations of the Canaanite world. To the west stretch the fertile plains leading to the Mediterranean Sea and the pleasures of the Philistines. Which would Samson choose? As we read the stories of his life, the answer becomes obvious.

To the west lies Timnath, where Samson killed a lion and married a Philistine woman against the advice of his parents; the vineyards, olive orchards, and grain fields Samson burned by setting the tails of 300 foxes on fire; Gaza, whose gates Samson carried away on his shoulders. To the west lived Delilah, whose seductive charms drew from Samson the secret of his great strength and the violation of the only covenant he had yet to break—the cutting of his hair. When Delilah shaved off the seven locks of his head "his strength went from him," and he became "weak . . . like any other man" (Judges 16:17,19).

Covenants make us strong. They keep us from the allures of a Philistine world. Without them we are like any other people. We must remember this as we roam the Sorek Valleys of our modern world. The scriptures admonish us to look to the east, to look to the hills of the Holy Land and the strength of a covenant life.

Samson played riddling games with the Philistines, loved and married their women, carried off the gates of their cities, slew them with the jawbone of an ass, and burned their fields. He had lived with the Philistines, and it is ironically appropriate that his last prayer would be, "Let me die with the Philistines." As we leave the Sorek Valley we are left to ponder . . . was Samson the strongest man in the Bible or the weakest?

RAVELING NORTH TO THE JEZREEL VALLEY, we make two stops where we may reflect upon the strength of others whose lives were recorded in the Book of Judges. In contrast to Samson, they were not mighty as to physical prowess; they were simple men and women, but they chose faith in the Lord, and their faith gave them spiritual power.

A climb to the top of Mt. Tabor is well worth the effort. Below stretches the beautiful Jezreel Valley. To the north lie the ruins of Hazor, the capital city of Jabin the Canaanite king who afflicted Israel during the time of Deborah. The captain of his army was Sisera, who commanded "nine hundred chariots of iron" (Judges 4:3). Deborah instructed Barak to gather the forces of Israel to Mt. Tabor and lead them in battle. How could ten thousand men under Barak's leadership stand against the armies and chariots of Sisera? "If thou wilt go with me," Barak answered Deborah, "then I will go: but if thou wilt not go with me, then will I not go. And she said, I will surely go with thee" (Judges 4:8-9).

I try to imagine myself in Barak's army, safely camped on the steep slopes of Tabor. Here no chariot can tear into the lines of assembled men. On the flat plains of Jezreel, however, who can stand against the fury of horses' hooves and chariot wheels? But Deborah is with us. We draw strength from the calm assurances of her faith. "Up," she commands, "for this is the day in which the Lord hath delivered Sisera into thine hand: is not the Lord gone out before thee? So Barak went down from Mt. Tabor, and ten thousand men after him" (Judges 4:14).

Climbing down the wooded slopes of Tabor, I can almost feel the anxiety in the mens' hearts as they prepare to face the chariots. They are "sent on foot into the valley" (Judges 5:15). Then the rains begin and increase to a downpour. The little brook Kishon overflows, flooding the plains and bogging down the chariot wheels. I imagine that Deborah smiled as the men watched, almost unbelieving, as Sisera fled.

The battle is over; the men sit at the foot of the mountain. If I close my eyes, I can almost hear the voices of Deborah and Barak as they sing to the gathered men. "Praise ye the Lord for the avenging of Israel, when the people willingly offered themselves . . . the stars in their courses fought against Sisera. The river of Kishon swept them away, that ancient river, . . . O my soul, thou hast trodden down strength" (Judges 5:2, 20-21). When we as a people "willingly offer ourselves" to the Lord's service, "the stars in heaven fight with us."

When the people willingly offered themselves . . . the stars in their courses fought against their enemies.

(Far Left) Mt. Tabor and the northeastern Jezreel Valley. Mt. Tabor is within sight of Nazareth and is a very prominent geogrpahical spot in the area. Perhaps the Savior came to its secluded slopes to ponder the ancient Old Testament stories he knew so well, and to commune with His Father in Heaven.

(Left) Sunset over the Jezreel Valley.

(Inset below) The wooded slopes of Mt. Tabor. Barak's army of ten thousand descended these slopes on foot to meet Sisera's army of chariots.

GENERATION LATER, the Lord would call a humble young man to deliver Israel from the Midianites. When addressed by the Lord as "thou mighty man of valour," Gideon replied, "Oh my Lord, wherewith shall I save Israel? Behold, my family is poor in Manasseh, and I am the least in my father's house" (Judges 6:12,15).

The Lord understands our weaknesses and fears and does what He can to reassure us. "If thou wilt save Israel by mine hand . . . I will put a fleece of wool in the floor; and if the dew be on the fleece only, and it be dry upon all the earth beside, then shall I know that thou wilt save Israel by mine hand" (Judges 6:36-37). In the morning the desired sign was

(Above) Gideon chooses his soldiers at the Spring of Harod. The Lord instructed Gideon to reduce the size of his army. "The Lord said unto Gideon, Every one that lappeth of the water with his tongue, as a dog lappeth, him shalt thou set by himself; likewise every- one that boweth down upon his knees to drink. And the number of them that lapped . . . were three hundred" (Judges 7:5-6).

(Right) En Harod, the Spring of Harod, in the late 19th century.

given. Gideon, still in need of assurance, asked the Lord to reverse the miracle. "And God did so that night: for it was dry upon the fleece only, and there was dew on all the ground" (Judges 6:40).

There are times in our lives when we need "fleeces" from the Lord. The challenges we face often seem too overwhelming, and we long to know the Lord is really with us or has truly asked us to perform them. How important those fleeces were for Gideon as he stared across the valley from his camp at the spring of Harod to the Hill of Moriah, where the Midianites "lay . . . like grasshoppers for multitude; and their camels were without number, as the sand by the sea side" (Judges 7:12).

The Lord would test Gideon's faith even further. "The people that are with thee are too many," the Lord said, and instructed Gideon to let all the fearful depart. Twenty-two thousand men left the camp. "The people are yet too many; bring them down unto the water, and I will try them for thee there" (Judges 7:2, 4).

I never tire of visiting the Spring of Harod and reading the story of Gideon while listening to the flowing water. Those who drew the water to their lips were allowed to remain. All the rest were sent home. Only three hundred stayed. "By the three hundred men . . . I will save you," the Lord promised (Judges 7:7). Like so many other stories in the Old Testament, this story has been preserved to teach us that when the Lord is with us, no enemy, be it physical or spiritual, can conquer us. As Jonathan would testify in a later gen-

eration, "There is no restraint to the Lord to save by many or by few" (1 Samuel 14:6).

Gideon waited for night to fall, gave each man a trumpet and a torch hidden within a pitcher, and positioned his three hundred men in a wide arc circling the Midianites on three sides. At a given signal, they broke the pitchers, revealing the lighted torches, blew their trumpets, and shouted, "The sword of the Lord and of Gideon. And they stood every man in his place" (Judges 7:20-21). As my eyes sweep over the plains where Gideon's men stood, the importance of those last eight words becomes clear. The combined strength of each of us standing firm in our place brings the victory. Confused and frightened by the suddenly appearing lights and the sound of three hundred trumpets, the Midianite army fled down the valley toward the Jordan River. Once again, the Lord demonstrated that weak and simple people of faith can overcome any opposition if they will but choose to serve the Lord.

(Above) Gideon's defeat of the Midianites is reminiscent of his ancestor Abraham's victory at Dan, when he divided his company of 318 men, and under cover of night, rescued Lot and his people from marauding kings. (See Gen. 14:14-15.) Gideon divided his 300 men into three groups, and gave each man a trumpet and pitcher that contained a lamp. Then, like all great commanders, he told them to follow his lead. They blew their trumpets, broke their pitchers, and with the lamps held aloft in their left hands cried, "The sword of the Lord and of Gideon." The Midianites were frightened into disarray, and a united army of Israel, led by a man whose faith in God never wavered, defeated them. (See Judges 7:16-21.)

Hannah was true to her vow, though it must have been painful.

Ruins of Shiloh. The ark of the covenant was lost when Eli's sons brought it from Shiloh during a battle with the Philistines. The Philistines placed it in a cart pulled by two milk cows. The cows then brought it to Beth Shemesh (1 Samuel 6:10-12). David would later place it in Jerusalem.

NORTH OF JERUSALEM, in the middle of rolling hills covered with olive vineyards, lie the ruins of ancient Shiloh. Here, for centuries, the tabernacle stood protecting the sacred Ark of the Covenant. From Shiloh, Joshua divided the land into each tribe's inheritance. For hundreds of years, in obedience to the law of Moses, the Israelites assembled to offer their sacrifices on the altar. From the top of a little hill where the tabernacle used to sit we can almost see the lines of worshippers gathering from every corner of the land. Among them all, the Lord chose to honor one woman by recording her story for posterity. She was a woman from the village of Ramah named Hannah.

Year after year, Hannah and her husband, Elkanah, journeyed to Shiloh to pay their devotions to Jehovah. But Hannah was a woman "in bitterness of soul . . . and of a sorrowful spirit," for she was barren. Imagine her thoughts as she approached the Lord's sanctuary, where she was determined to "[pour] out [her] soul before the Lord" (1 Samuel 1:10,15). Standing before the tabernacle, assured that the Lord she worshiped would help those who came to Him, she "vowed a vow, and said, O Lord of hosts, if thou wilt indeed look on the affliction of thine handmaid, and remember me, and not forget thine handmaid, but wilt give unto thine handmaid a man child, then I will give him unto the Lord all the days of his life." Having left her sorrow in the hands of her God, Hannah "went her way . . . and her countenance was no more sad." (See 1 Samuel 1:11,18.)

Her faith was rewarded. The Lord *did* remember her and sent into her care a baby boy whom she named Samuel. He would become one of the Lord's great prophets and the last judge of Israel. As I read her story on the very spot where she prayed, I feel the great responsibility of parenthood. I too longed for children, and the Lord has been gracious. I seem to feel Hannah's spirit and the power of her vow—to return the longed-for child back to the Lord. Perhaps the Lord would have all of us make that same promise. Into our care, He sends His precious children. "Train them in such a way that they will return to me," He seems to say.

Hannah was true to her vow, though it must have been painful. I marvel at the magnitude of her sacrifice. "When she had weaned him, she took him up with her . . . and brought him unto the house of the Lord in Shiloh: and the child was young. . . . For this child I prayed; and the Lord hath given me my petition . . . Therefore, also I have lent him to the Lord; as long as he liveth he shall be lent to the Lord" (1 Samuel 1:24,27-28).

Hannah placed her only son into the hands of Eli, the high priest, then turned and walked down the slope of Shiloh; but each year she returned to see her son and bring him the "little coat" she had made for him. I can imagine no greater gift of devotion, no greater sacrifice of a mother. Perhaps, like Abraham, she too understood the heart of our Father in Heaven when He sent His well-beloved Son into the world.

ThY SERVANT heARETh

I am moved by another thought that comes whenever I stand on the ground where the ancient tabernacle once rested. One night, as the boy Samuel lay in the darkness, the Lord called his name. Unaccustomed to the whisperings of the Spirit, three times Samuel thought it was Eli's voice. When he finally knew it was the Lord calling his name, Samuel responded, "Speak; for thy servant heareth" (1 Samuel 3:10). This is the submissive, willing answer the Lord searches for in His prophets before they begin their ministry. This surrender to the Lord's will is evident in almost every prophet in the Old Testament.

While in the temple, Isaiah heard the Lord ask, "Who will go for us?" And he responded, "Here am I: send me" (Isaiah 6:8). We hear echoes of the Savior's own words in the premortal existence as we contemplate Isaiah's response to the Lord's call. As I walk the ground where Samuel gave himself to his God, I wonder if I am responding to the Lord's calls with that same sweet submission. Are we not invited to walk in the Lord's tabernacle today? In those holy places, do we not hear the Lord call our name, anticipating the same consecrating obedience in our voice as He heard in theirs? Should we not all say, "Speak, Lord; for thy servant heareth?"

The Lord's Anointed Kings

Everywhere you travel in the Holy Land, you see the pale green foliage of olive trees. The land is literally covered with them. When I first came to the Holy Land I did not think the olive a very beautiful tree, but when I came to understand the power of its symbolism, I saw the olive tree with new eyes. To this day, the olive leaf suggests peace. The oil pressed from its fruit brought light to ancient homes, and both the leaves and the oil were linked with healing. Peace—Light—Healing. All these uses are associated with the Holy Spirit. The olive tree was a symbol of the nation of Israel itself. Olive oil burning in the tabernacle suggested that God's house was illuminated with the light of the Holy Ghost. Was not the Lord teaching them that they must be full of the Spirit so they could bring light, peace, and healing to the world?

Olive trees at the traditional site of Gethsemane.

Inset: Olive tree blossom.

HREE MAIN CALLINGS in the Old Testament required anointing with oil—kings, priests, and prophets. These were the Lord's chosen, and pouring olive oil on their heads suggested that no man had the right to officiate in a leadership position, be it political or religious, unless he was filled with the Spirit.

While cooling my feet in the pools at En-gedi, I think of the power in the simple act of pouring oil on a man, and the tremendous respect it generated. When Israel demanded that Samuel provide them with a king that they "may be like all the nations," (1 Samuel 8:20) the Lord instructed Samuel to anoint Saul, "a choice young man, and a goodly: and there was not among the children of Israel a goodlier person than he" (1 Samuel 9:2). While pouring a vial of oil on Saul's head, Samuel promised him, "the Spirit of the Lord will come upon thee, and thou . . . shalt be turned into another man" (1 Samuel 10:6).

Three main callings required annointing with oil— kings, priests, and prophets.

(Opposite page) Olive press at BYU Jerusalem Center.

(Inset opposite page) Olive press at Capernaum.

(Left) Shepherd's Hill looking toward Bethlehem. David was anointed king by Samuel in Bethlehem. The Lord said to Samuel, "Look not on his countenance, or on the height of his stature; . . . for the Lord seeth not as man seeth; for man looketh on the outward appearance, but the Lord looketh on the heart" (1 Samuel 16:7).

David would not stretch forth his hand against the anointed of the Lord.

(Left) Falls at En-gedi. En-gedi is located on the western shore of the Dead Sea. It was here that David and his men hid from Saul.

BUT SAUL LOST THE SPIRIT through his disobedience and his obsession with killing David. Here, by the waterfalls of En-gedi, Saul entered a cave to rest from his pursuit. As fate would have it, David and his men were hiding in the darkness of the cavern. His men urged David to slay Saul, but David hesitated, cutting "the skirt of Saul's robe privily," instead. The severed portion symbolized Saul's authority. "And it came to pass afterward that David's heart smote him, because he had cut off Saul's skirt. And he said to his men, The Lord forbid that I should do this thing unto my master, the Lord's anointed, to stretch forth mine hand against him, seeing he is the anointed of the Lord" (1 Samuel 24:4-6).

David's respect for Saul, unworthy though Saul was, never wavered. I wonder whether my own respect for the Lord's anointed today is equal with that of David. Similar thoughts come while on a field near Bethlehem. Here, Samuel traveled at the command of the Lord to anoint David as king of Israel. As soon as the oil was poured on David's head, "the Spirit of the Lord came upon David from that day forward. . . . But the Spirit of the Lord departed from Saul" (1 Samuel 16:13-14).

Charity . . . seeketh not her own.

JONACHAN

Even though time is usually short when visiting the Holy Land, I always feel obligated to stop at Beit Shean. I must pay my respects to an old friend. Beit Shean was a Philistine stronghold during the days of Saul, and only one thing of Biblical significance took place here. After the Battle of Mt. Gilboa, the victorious Philistines hung the headless bodies of Saul and Jonathan from the city walls. There is nothing left but a huge mound and the ruins of a subsequent Roman settlement to mark the site of this Old Testament city; but, like a mourner putting flowers on a grave, I never fail to think of Jonathan when I pass by. There are few people in the Bible I love more than this noble son of Saul. He was as courageous as David, for he and his armor bearer defeated a whole garrison of Philistines alone, confident they would receive the Lord's protective care. Though denied his place as Israel's next king by Samuel's anointing of David, Jonathan remained loyal to David till his death. In spite of Saul's reminders that David stood in his way of obtaining the kingdom, Jonathan defended David, warned David, strengthened David. He even placed his own "garments, even to his sword, and to his bow, and to his girdle," upon David, symbolizing that David would replace Jonathan as king, for he "loved him as his own soul" (1 Samuel 18:3-4).

Paul's definition of charity contains the words, "Charity . . . seeketh not her own" (1 Corinthians 13:5). If I could write an epitaph to place on the walls of Beit Shean they would contain Paul's words, for surely no man lived a higher standard of charity than did Jonathan. He died with his father, remaining true to both men he loved.

(Top) Tel Beit Shean hill.

(Bottom) Tel Beit Shean ruins. It was here that the Philistines hung the headless bodies of Saul and his sons on the city walls. The men of Jabesh-gilead came in the night "and took the body of Saul and the bodies of his sons from the wall . . . and came to Jabesh, and burnt them there. And they took their bones, and buried them under a tree at Jabesh" (1 Samuel 31:12-13).

the KINGS of ISRAEL

(Left) The wickedness of these kings caused the Lord to send many prophets to call them to repentance.

(Below) With the death of Solomon, the kingdom split into two nations, Judah in the south, and ten tribes (called Israel) in the north led by the tribe of Ephraim—a tragic division of Jehovah's covenant people—but Isaiah prophesied of a future day when "Ephraim shall not envy Judah, and Judah shall not vex Ephraim" (Isaiah 11:13). Ezekiel also saw the time when "they shall be no more two nations, neither shall they be divided into two kingdoms anymore at all . . . and they shall have one shepherd" (Ezek. 37:22, 24).

Jeroboam was the first king of divided Israel. He set up image worship at Dan and Bethel (two calves supposedly representing Jehovah), which earned him the rebuke of the prophet Ahijah. Jeroboam went on to make priests of men who were not of the family of Aaron, and instituted the worship of graven images.

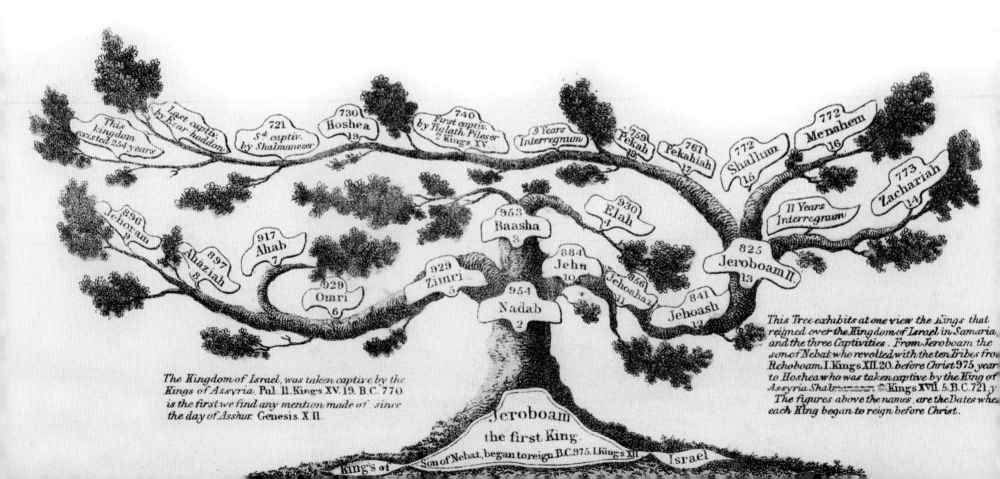

This kingdom existed 254 years

Last captiv. by Esar haddon

721 3d captiv. by Shalmaneser

730 Hoshea 19

740 First captiv. by Tiglath Pileser 2 Kings XV

9 Years Interregnum

759 Pekah 19

761 Pekahiah 17

772 Shallum 15

772 Menahem 16

773 Zachariah 14

896 Jehoram 9

897 Ahaziah 8

917 Ahab 7

929 Omri 6

929 Zimri 5

953 Baasha 3

954 Nadab 2

930 Elah 4

884 Jehu 10

856 Jehoahaz 11

841 Jehoash 12

11 Years Interregnum

825 Jeroboam II. 13

The Kingdom of Israel, was taken captive by the Kings of Assyria. Pul. II.Kings XV.19. B.C.770. is the first we find any mention made of, since the day of Asshur. Genesis. X.II.

This Tree exhibits at one view the Kings that reigned over the Kingdom of Israel in Samaria, and the three Captivities. From Jeroboam the son of Nebat who revolted with the ten Tribes from Rehoboam. I.Kings XII.20. before Christ 975 years to Hoshea who was taken captive by the King of Assyria Shalmaneser. 2 Kings XVII. 5. B.C.721 y
The figures above the names, are the Dates when each King began to reign before Christ.

Jeroboam the first King

King's of Son of Nebat, began to reign B.C.975. I.Kings XII Israel

the KINGS of JUDAH

(Below) Though the Kingdom of Israel experienced wicked, idolatrous, and rebellious kings up to their captivity and scattering by the Assyrians, Judah (led by David's descendants) enjoyed the enlightened rule of a number of exceptional kings. Many of them had great messages to teach as they shared their faith with their people.

Jehosephat said, "Believe in the Lord your God, so shall ye be established; believe his prophets so shall ye prosper" (2 Chron. 20:20). Hezekiah was granted 15 more years of life when he prayed, "Remember now, O Lord, I beseech thee, how I have walked before thee in truth and with a perfect heart, and have done that which is good in thy sight"

(Isaiah 38:3). "Thou hast in love to my soul delivered it from the pit of corruption: for thou hast cast all my sins behind thy back" (Isaiah 38:17).

Josiah encouraged the priesthood of his day with these words: "prepare yourselves . . . and stand in the holy place. . . . And sanctify yourselves, and prepare your brethren, that they may do according to the word of the Lord" (2 Chron. 35:4-6).

Asa, during a time of crisis, "cried unto the Lord his God, and said, Lord, it is nothing with thee to help, whether with many, or with them that have no power: help us, O Lord our God; for we rest on thee" (2 Chron. 14:11).

(Right) Rehoboam succeeds his father, Solomon, as king of Israel and was crowned in Shechem. He showed poor political judgment, however, when he increased the already rigorous financial burdens Solomon had placed upon the people, and the kingdom of Israel divided during his reign (1 Kgs. 12).

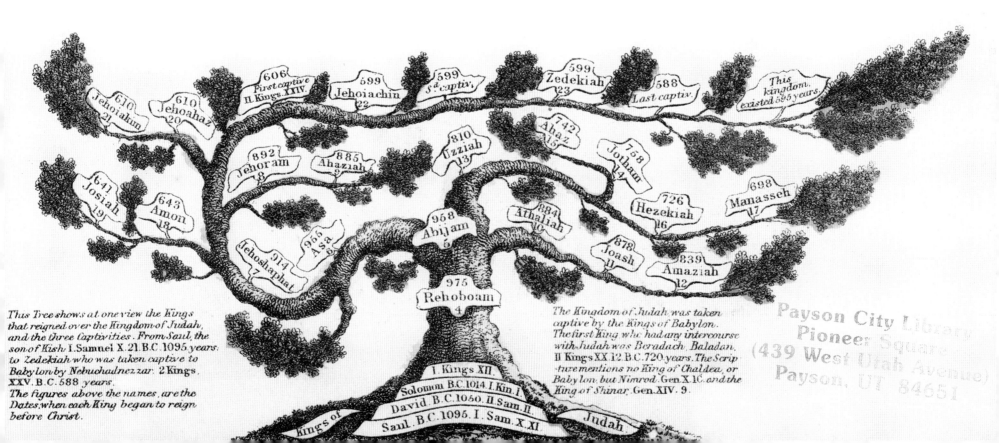

610 Jehoiakun 21

610 Jehoahaz 20

606 First captive II. Kings. XXIV.

599 Jehoiachin 22

599 3.d captiv.

599 Zedekiah 23

588 Last captiv.

This kingdom existed 595 years.

742 Ahaz 15

810 Uzziah 13

758 Jotham 14

892 Jehoram 8

885 Ahaziah 9

726 Hezekiah 16

698 Manasseh 17

641 Josiah 19

643 Amon 18

955 Asa 6

958 Abijam 5

884 Athaliah 10

914 Jehoshaphat 7

878 Joash 11

839 Amaziah 12

975 Rehoboam 4

This Tree shows at one view the Kings that reigned over the Kingdom of Judah, and the three Captivities. From Saul, the son of Kish I. Samuel X. 21. B.C. 1095 years: to Zedekiah who was taken captive to Babylon by Nebuchadnezzar. 2 Kings. XXV. B.C. 588 years.
The figures above the names, are the Dates, when each King began to reign before Christ.

I. Kings XII.
Solomon B.C. 1014 I. Kin. I.
David B.C. 1050. II. Sam. II.
Saul B.C. 1095. I. Sam. X. XI.

kings of Judah

The Kingdom of Judah was taken captive by the Kings of Babylon. The first King who had any intercourse with Judah was Beradach Baladan, II Kings XX 12. B.C. 720 years. The Scripture mentions no King of Chaldea, or Babylon but Nimrod. Gen. X. 10. and the King of Shinar. Gen. XIV. 9.

a RMED WITH THE STRENGTH OF THE SPIRIT, David traveled to the Valley of Elah to bring supplies to his brothers. There he heard the mocking voice of Goliath defying the God of Israel. As I walk along the brook where David chose "five smooth stones," the realization of the source of David's strength comes forcefully to me. And I understand why Saul was afraid to face the giant Philistine, even though he was the tallest man in Israel—and their king. The Spirit of the Lord fills one with the courage necessary to face any opposition we may encounter in life. What was true then is true now.

Most people who walk up the brook in the Valley of Elah choose their own five smooth stones. I am no different. While I finger them, I can hear a voice from the past, filled with the Spirit, speaking words of testimony and faith. "Thou comest to me with a sword, and with a spear, and with a shield: but I come to thee in the name of the Lord of hosts . . . This day will the Lord deliver thee into mine hand . . . that all the earth may know that there is a God in Israel" (1 Samuel 17:45-46).

Placing one of my chosen stones in my own sling, I throw it as far as I can. A scripture comes to mind and I know that David was armed with more than these stones. He carried into battle a sword more powerful than that of Goliath's. "Take . . . the sword of my Spirit, which I will pour out upon you" (D&C 27:18). That sword continues to defend the Lord's children to this day.

(Far left) Sling and stones from the Valley of Elah. The sling was a formidable weapon. We read that 700 left-handed men of the tribe of Benjamin "could sling stones at an hair breadth, and not miss" (Judges 20:16).

(Left) Rocks in a dry streambed in the Valley of Elah. The story of David's defeat of Goliath in the Valley of Elah has become one of the best loved and inspiring stories of the Old Testament. When Michelangelo needed an image to represent the spirit of the Renaissance and the dignity of man, he sculpted David at his moment of confrontation in the Valley of Elah.

(Right) The Valley of Elah, which is located twenty miles southwest of Jerusalem. Inspired by the courage of David's victory here, the rest of Israel pushed down the slopes, chasing the fleeing Philistines. Often, one person's courage can instill in the hearts of others the faith necessary to rise to the challenge of their own Philistine foes.

"Give . . . thy servant an understanding heart . . . that I may discern between good and bad" (1 Kings 3:9).

(Right) The Gihon Spring is the main water source of the city of Jerusalem, and lies at the entrance to Hezekiah's water tunnel. As the life of cities were determined by the presence of water, Jerusalem's location was determined by this spring. During various times in Jerusalem's history, different means were used to secure this water source.

THESE THOUGHTS LEAD US next to Jerusalem, chosen by David as his new capital. Each time I go to Jerusalem I visit the Gihon Spring. It is the main water source of the city and explains why Jerusalem is situated where it is. Here another anointing took place. Just before he died, David instructed Nathan, the prophet, and Zadok, the high priest, to take his son Solomon to this place and "anoint him there king over Israel" (1 Kings 1:34). What would the Spirit do for Solomon?

We travel north of Jerusalem to the little village of Gibeon— a peaceful place, one fit for the Lord to reveal Himself to His newly anointed king. "In Gibeon the Lord appeared to Solomon in a dream by night: . . . Ask what I shall give thee" (1 Kings 3:5). Here on the same ground where Solomon offered his sacrifices, I sense that Solomon's request was guided by the Holy Ghost. Are we not taught that the Spirit will help us in our prayers and fill us with desire for the right things? "I am but a little child. . . . Give therefore thy servant an understanding heart to judge thy people, that I may discern between good and bad" (1 Kings 3:7, 9).

It is pleasant to sit here and read the stories and proverbs testifying to the wisdom the Lord bestows on His people through the Holy Spirit.

We can still hear the voice of kingly wisdom speaking to us here in the shade of Gibeon. "Trust in the Lord with all thine heart; and lean not unto thine own understanding" (Proverbs 3:5). "Where no counsel is, the people fall: but in the multitude of counselors there is safety" (Proverbs 11:14). "Righteousness exalteth a nation: but sin is a reproach to any people" (Proverbs 14:34). "A soft answer turneth away wrath . . ." (Proverbs 15:1). "Before honour is humility . . ." (Proverbs 15:33). "A merry heart doeth good like a medicine" (Proverbs 17:22). "A good name is rather to be chosen than great riches" (Proverbs 22:1). "Train up a child in the way he should go: and when he is old, he will not depart from it" (Proverbs 22:6). "Who can find a virtuous woman? for her price is far above rubies" (Proverbs 31:10). "To everything there is a season, and a time to every purpose under the heaven" (Ecclesiastes 3:1). "Live joyfully with the wife whom thou lovest all the days of the life of thy vanity . . . for that is thy portion in this life" (Ecclesiastes 9:9). "The race is not to the swift, nor the battle to the strong . . ." (Ecclesiastes 9:11). These are the types of truths the Holy Spirit can still impart to us if we learn to listen to its soft whisper.

David also was gifted through the Spirit to write beautiful words. His choice of expression was the psalm or hymn. We learn a great deal about the soul of a man by what he creates. The Psalms tell us much about David, and in turn about the Hebrew people, for David sang with their voice. Solomon built the first temple, but David expressed the Spirit's testimony of its beauty and the longing of the human soul for its healing power.

Though no temple has stood on the Temple Mount for close to two thousand years, I still sense a feeling of holiness when I walk across the stones where it once stood. David's words seem to express my own thoughts and love for the Lord's house. "One thing have I desired of the Lord, that will I seek after; that I may dwell in the house of the Lord all the days of my life, to behold the beauty of the Lord, and to enquire in his temple" (Psalms 27:4). "We shall be satisfied with the goodness of thy house, even of thy holy temple" (Psalms 65:4). "My soul longeth, yea, even fainteth for the courts of the Lord: . . . For a day in thy courts is better than a thousand. I had rather be a doorkeeper in the house of my God, than to dwell in the tents of wickedness" (Psalms 84:2,10).

(Above) Solomon builds a temple. Solomon's Temple was later rebuilt by Zerubbabel when the Jews returned from Babylonian captivity. Herod completely remodeled the temple in New Testament times.

(Left) Herod's Temple in the model city in Jerusalem. The Dome of the Rock was built on this same spot, where Muslims believe Mohammed was taken into heaven, and Christians and Jews regard it as the location where Abraham was asked to sacrifice Isaac.

(Above) Looking over the shoulder of an Orthodox Jew at the Western Wall in Jerusalem.

(Right) A Jewish man stands and recites prayers at the Western Wall. This wall is the most significant place in Jerusalem for religious Jews today. It is a remnant of the ancient temple enclosure that supported the Temple Mount during the reign of Herod the Great. The Lord told Moses He would meet and commune with him from the Holy of Holies in the temple. The Western Wall is near where the ancient temple stood. Today, people will not only pray here, but many write their prayers on little papers and leave them in the cracks between stones in the wall.

I HAVE OFTEN STOOD next to the Western Wall and watched the reverence the Jewish people have for their lost temple. Here they come to pray, to lovingly touch the stones that represent a day of former glory, and to spend a few moments in quiet reflection. As I witness both their grief at the loss of their ancient temple, and their joy at being so close to where it once stood, the Spirit seems to whisper, "You possess what they lost. Is your enjoyment of modern temples, with all their fullness of ordinances, equal to their sorrow?"

The Spirit also put into the soul of David an abiding love for the scriptures. While in Jerusalem, every Thursday morning we come to the Western Wall to witness the bar mitzvahs. They are happy, celebratory affairs. In Judaism, a boy is a man when he can recite and expound the sacred texts of his forefathers. These moments of joy are deeply moving to those of us who witness them. I watch them kiss the Torah scrolls and hold them lovingly in their hands. Fathers, uncles, grandfathers, and brothers surround each boy as he performs the rite of passage into manhood. Mothers trill their joy with high-pitched voices, and

(Above) A young Jewish boy reciting from the Torah at his Bar Mitzvah ceremony held at the Western Wall, Jerusalem.

throw candy to symbolize the sweetness of the moment. In this joy, the spirit of the Psalms is felt. I open my Bible and read, "Thy testimonies also are my delight and my counsellors. . . . Oh how love I thy law! It is my meditation all the day. . . . Thy word is a lamp unto my feet, and a light unto my path. . . . Great peace have they which love thy law: and nothing shall offend them" (Psalms 119:24, 97, 105, 165).

To David, the words of the Lord were "more to be desired . . . than gold, yea, than much fine gold: sweeter also than honey and the honeycomb" (Psalms 19:10). In these celebrations of gladness, we hear the happiness of the Psalms once again as David lives on in the new manhood of his sons.

As we witness the living spirit of the Psalms and realize the fulness that we, ourselves, have been given, we can understand the Psalmist's words when he wrote, "I love the Lord . . . because he hath inclined his ear unto me, therefore will I call upon him as long as I live. . . . Return unto thy rest, O my soul; for the Lord hath dealt bountifully with thee. . . . What shall I render unto the Lord for all his benefits toward me?" (Psalms 116:1, 2, 7, 12). Each of us must answer this question for ourselves.

A S THE SUN SETS OVER JERUSALEM, my thoughts of Saul, and David, and Solomon end in a sad reflection. These anointed men, so filled with the Spirit, who wrote and taught many wonderful things that have enriched my life, all made fateful choices that drove the Spirit from them. Saul, obsessed with power, forgot the humility of his youth, "played the fool," (1 Samuel 26:21) and ended his days at the feet of the witch of En-dor. David's surrendering moments with Bathsheba, his ordering of Uriah to his death, and his witnessing of the tragic choices of his children wrung from his soul some of the most painful words we read in the Old Testament. Solomon, though builder of the first temple to Jehovah, nevertheless succumbed to the influence of his many foreign wives and amassed wealth, and built shrines to the false gods of the world. So their decisions become a warning for my own. If men of this spiritual stature can fall, all of us need to watch our lives closely. The Spirit of the Lord is a precious gift, but it must be heeded at all times, in all circumstances, and until the end of life. May all our decisions reflect its wisdom, love, and commitment to truth and righteousness.

As I turn from the temple mount and gaze at the ever-present olive trees, I feel again the appropriateness of their presence in the Holy Land. This is indeed a land filled with the Spirit; a Spirit that has ever blessed those who walked it; a Spirit that continues to give peace, healing, and light.

IN THE LANDS OF EXILE

Today for the first time in many trips to the Holy Land, I am able to visit Samaria, the capital of the northern kingdom of Israel. We are in the West Bank, which has been closed to visitors for many years. Conditions on this day make it possible to stand on this hilltop city and reflect on the scattering of Israel, which began at this spot and would continue for many generations until the Romans would complete the job a few decades after the resurrection of the Savior.

Looking between trees at a field in Samaria.

Inset: Stone tablet dating back to the first century.

THE SCENERY IS SO PEACEFUL and beautiful, with a warm breeze blowing, that it is hard to imagine the slopes below me covered with Assyrian chariots, armed men, and siege towers. Eventually the city would fall and the ten tribes would be carried from their homeland to be resettled throughout the Assyrian empire. They never returned, and to this day we remember them as the lost ten tribes. I experience a strange emotion. I am a descendant of Ephraim, and my own ancestors began their long journey of exile from this spot. In time they would find new homelands in the north. How many generations did it take before they became lost to themselves, forgetting their ancient homeland and the stories of their forefathers? Here at Samaria, I begin to comprehend the homesickness I feel each time I leave the shores of this land.

From the Mt. of Olives, I can look down upon the Old City of Jerusalem. In another generation, the remaining tribe of Judah watched as their beloved Jerusalem was destroyed and their temple leveled by the Babylonians. From their place of exile they would lament, "By the rivers of Babylon, there we sat down, yea, we wept, when we remembered Zion. . . . For there they that carried us away captive required of us a song; . . . How shall we sing the Lord's song in a strange land? If I forget thee, O Jerusalem, let my right hand forget her cunning. If I do not remember thee, let my tongue cleave to the roof of my mouth; if I prefer not Jerusalem above my chief joy" (Psalms 137:1-6).

Mt. of Olives. Zechariah prophesied of the most dramatic and emotional moment in the long history of this sacred mountain, a moment that awaits the second coming of the Lord. "And his feet shall stand in that day upon the mount of Olives . . . and the mount of Olives shall cleave in the midst thereof toward the east and toward the west, and there shall be a very great valley; and half of the mountain shall remove toward the north, and half of it toward the south" (Zech. 14:4). "And one shall say unto him, What are these wounds in thine hands? Then he shall answer, "Those with which I was wounded in the house of my friends" (Zech. 13:6).

(Opposite page) Looking down on Old City Jerusalem.

MOSES PROPHESIED OF THE SCATTERING OF ISRAEL and how they would be treated in the lands of their exile. Before they even crossed the Jordan River, he said: "Thou shalt grope at noonday, as the blind gropeth in darkness, and thou shalt not prosper in thy ways: and thou shalt be only oppressed and spoiled evermore, and no man shall save thee. . . . And among these nations shalt thou find no ease, neither shall the sole of thy foot have rest: but the Lord shall give thee there a trembling heart, and failing of eyes, and sorrow of mind: And thy life shall hang in doubt before thee; and thou shalt fear day and night, and shalt have none assurance of thy life: In the morning thou shalt say, Would God it were even! and at even thou shalt say, Would God it were morning! for the fear of thine heart wherewith thou shalt fear, and for the sight of thine eyes which thou shalt see" (Deuteronomy 28:29, 65-67).

I read these sobering lines outside Yad Vashem, the Holocaust memorial in Jerusalem, and think of the suffering the Jewish people have endured in the lands of exile. It is always a difficult visit, especially the children's memorial where mirrors reflect millions of candles stretching out to the farthest limits of sight. Each candle represents a child killed in the concentration camps of Nazi Germany. I have walked, weeping, through the showers and crematoriums of Dachau.

Here one is forced to wrestle with the question of human suffering and meaningless evil on an immense scale. Where do we turn to understand, and somehow find the strength to endure and resist this mystery of human pain, as old as life itself?

There is a sculpture at Yad Vashem consisting of the emaciated skeletal bodies of the Holocaust victims. They remind me of another man who, plagued with a loathsome disease, stripped of everything he possessed, mourning for the loss of his dead children, mocked and despised by those around him, and tormented by nightmares that robbed him of sleep, sat on an ash heap in the land of Uz and asked God, "WHY?" "My bone cleaveth to my skin and my flesh," he said, "And I am escaped with the skin of my teeth. Have pity on me, have pity on me . . ." (Job 19:20-21).

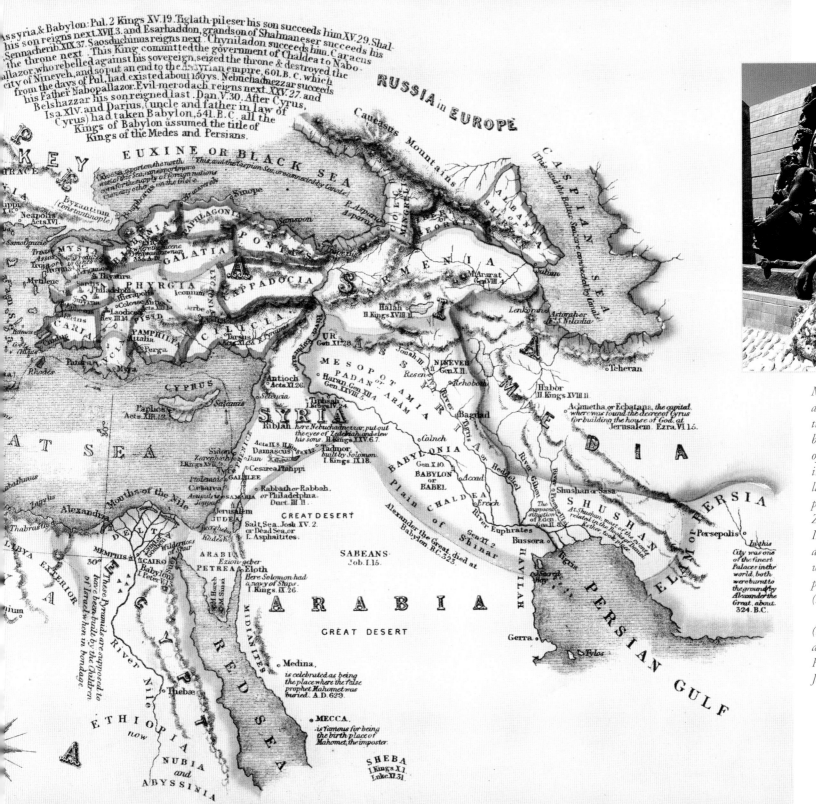

Map portraying the land
as it was divided during
the time of exile and
bondage. The scattering
of Israel was also a blessing of the Lord upon the
lands where his chosen
people would go.
Zephaniah stated that
Israel "will get praise
and fame in every land
where they have been
put to shame"
(Zeph 3:19)

(Inset above) Sculpture
at Yad Vashem
Holocaust Memorial in
Jerusalem.

IN THE WISDOM OF THE OLD TESTAMENT we find the story of Job. Satan, "the accuser of our brethren . . . which accused them before our God day and night," (Revelation 12:10) confronted God about the devotion of His children. They are only righteous; they only love and serve Jehovah when He is good to them, but in the midst of suffering and confronted with inexplicable evil, they will surely curse the very God they profess to worship. Job's "comforter" friends sit down with him and try to make sense of the disaster of his life. Since God is just, they reason, Job has sinned. He is deserving of the evil that has befallen him. But Job maintains his integrity.

Evil on the scale of the Holocaust cannot be explained away with the simple logic of Job's accusing friends, armed with their moral formulas and truisms about God. Yet from the depths of his suffering, Job throws Satan's challenge back into his teeth by saying, "The Lord gave, and the Lord hath taken away; blessed be the name of the Lord" (Job 1:21). Job obtains an answer from God, which in truth is not an answer that satisfies us and yet, perhaps, it is the only answer God can give.

(Above) Job discovered that all he had was lost or destroyed as one servant after another arrived to tell him of another disaster. Through all of these afflictions, however, Job did not curse God's name, nor turn away from him. (See Book of Job 1:13-22.)

(Left) Silhouette of trees and people on the ridge of Shepherd's Field in Israel.

"Where wast thou when I laid the foundations of the earth? declare if thou hast understanding. When the morning stars sang together, and all the sons of God shouted for joy?" (Job 38:4, 7). This is followed by question after question regarding the laws of creation. Because our knowledge is so limited and our life on earth so brief, we cannot begin to comprehend even the most elementary aspects of the mind of God and His designs in the creation of man.

No people have suffered like scattered Israel. Decade after decade, century after century, through the pogroms and the massacres, the Jewish people have continued to deny the accusation of Lucifer. From the ash heaps of Dachau, reduced to Job's bone and skin, they bowed before their God, affirming what their ancestors have asserted through two thousand years of Job-like sorrow, "Hear, O Israel: The Lord our God is one Lord: And thou shalt love the Lord thy God with all thine heart, and with all thy soul, and with all thy might" (Deuteronomy 6:4-5). God's answer to unconscionable evil and human suffering is the continued devotion of His scattered people who persist in testifying, "I know that my redeemer liveth, . . . and though after my skin worms destroy this body, yet in my flesh shall I see God" (Job 19:25-26). What would the world be like if the iron grip of evil were ever so great that Satan's challenge rang true and mankind turned his eyes heavenward to "curse God and die" (Job 2:9)?

THE LORD WOULD CONTINUE to be mindful of His people, though they were separated from their homeland. In the midst of Babylon, or facing the hatred of a Haman, God would send them Daniels and Esthers to bring "enlargement and deliverance" (Esther 4:14) and hope in their future destiny.

Did not the Lord tell Hosea, "When Israel was a child, then I loved him . . . . How shall I give thee up, Ephraim? How shall I deliver thee, Israel? My heart is turned toward thee, and my mercies are extended to gather thee" (Hosea 11:1, 8 JST). Though Israel believed God had "forsaken . . . and forgotten" them, Isaiah wrote, "Can a woman forget her sucking child, that she should not have compassion on the son of her womb? yea, they may forget, yet will I not forget thee" (Isaiah 49:14-15).

The stories of captive, scattered Israel are all stories of hope. Even in exile one must be strong and remain true. Shadrach, Meshach, and Abed-Nego refused to bow before the idols of Babylon. When the music sounded, demanding submission, they remained standing. As a child I loved this story. I pictured the three young men standing boldly in the midst of hundreds of others who fell to their knees at the given signal. Carried before the king, and threatened with death, they replied, "Our God whom we serve is able to deliver us from the burning fiery furnace, and he will deliver us out of thine hand, O king. But if not, be it

known unto thee, O king, that we will not serve thy gods, nor worship the golden image which thou hast set up" (Daniel 3:17-18).

When they were thrown into the furnace, protection came. "Lo, I see four men loose, walking in the midst of the fire," Nebuchadnezzar said, "and they have no hurt; and the form of the fourth is like the Son of God" (Daniel 3:25).

The golden images of the world are often compelling. When the music of modern Babylon sounds in our ears, do we bow with the rest of the world, lest our different standards and values cause us to stand conspicuously alone? The message is plain. If we will resist the temptation to bow with the world, we may walk with Christ. Perhaps these young men found their courage in the

The stories of captive and scattered Israel are stories of hope.

words of Isaiah, who wrote, "When thou walkest through the fire, thou shalt not be burned . . . . for I am the Lord thy God . . . . Since thou wast precious in my sight, . . . and I have loved thee" (Isaiah 43:2-4).

Daniel, too, was protected—not because he was of the chosen seed of Abraham, but, as Darius the king knew, "Thy God whom thou servest continually, he will deliver thee" (Daniel 6:16). Daniel was also aware of the reason he was saved in the lions' den. "My God hath sent his angel, and hath shut the lions' mouths," he told Darius, "forasmuch as before him innocency was found in me . . ." (Daniel 6:22). Though we are a Zion people living in an alien world, the Lord expects our innocence and continuous service.

(Opposite page) Esther reveals Haman's plot to destroy the Jews. Knowing she needed the prayers and faith of her people, Esther asked Mordecai to "Go, gather together all the Jews that are present in Shushan, and fast ye for me, and neither eat nor drink three days, night or day: . . . and so will I go in unto the king, which is not according to the law: and if I perish, I perish" (Esther 4:16).

(Opposite page) Shadrach, Meshach, and Abed-Nego are delivered from the burning furnace. When Nebuchadnezzar saw the Lord's protecting power manifested in behalf of Shadrach, Meshach, and Abed-Nego, he praised their God and marvelled at these men of integrity. (See Daniel 3:28.)

(Left) Daniel is spared in the lions' den. Darius, deeply impressed with the integrity of Daniel, and with Jehovah's loving protection, issued a decree stating that "the God of Daniel . . . is the living God, . . . and his kingdom that which shall not be destroyed" (Daniel 6:26).

NOTHER THOUGHT SUSTAINS chosen Israel in the lands of captivity. There is a beautiful mosaic floor in the ruins of Sepphoris in Galilee. It contains images of various wild animals of ancient Israel—lions, bears, leopards. Though they are ferocious images, I feel hope as I study them. I sit in the shade looking at the mosaics and read of Daniel's dream. He was shown a lion, a bear, a leopard, and a "terrible beast." Each represented a new empire that would rise up and dominate Israel. Babylon, the lion—Persia, the bear—Greece, the leopard—and Rome, the terrible beast, would devour the smaller, weaker nations around them. Predatory in nature, they would establish the rule of conquest through power. It has ever been this way, I think, and continues to this day. I read on, and Daniel's words take me back to America, to the state of Missouri, to a place called Adam-ondi-Ahman.

Here the rolling hills and broad valley floor instill peace. In vision, Daniel saw this place and prophesied. "The beasts . . . had their dominion taken away: yet their lives were prolonged for a season and time. I saw in the night visions, and one like the Son of man came with the clouds of heaven, and came to the Ancient of days, [Adam] and they brought him near before him. And there was given him dominion, and glory, and a kingdom, that all people, nations, and languages, should serve him: his dominion is an everlasting dominion which shall not pass away" (Daniel 7:12-14).

If I lift my eyes from the mosaic beasts, I can see sheep grazing on the hillside. Will the weak and defenseless ever live in peace with the mighty and the predatory? Isaiah has the answer and here, by the floor of Sepphoris, I come to understand the deeper meaning of his words. In the Savior's everlasting kingdom, "The wolf also shall dwell with the lamb, and the leopard shall lie down with the kid; and the calf and the young lion . . . and a little child shall lead them, . . . their young ones shall lie down together . . . and the sucking child shall play on the hole of the asp" (Isaiah 11:6-8). How many times, I think, have I read these verses and applied them only literally? Now I comprehend. There will be a time when the mighty nations will live in peace with the defenseless ones. There will be a time when those as innocent and trusting as a child will not be victims to the cunning, the sly, and the deceitful. There will be a time when one generation will not pass down its hatreds, angers, and prejudices to their descendants. The children will "lie down together in harmony." In this Holy Land, which has seen so much violence and anger over the centuries, Isaiah's prophecy brings assurance of a joyful future.

(Below) Old City Jerusalem seen from Orson Hyde Memorial Garden. Jerusalem has always been able to instill a deep love in those who know her. The Lord Himself said that Jerusalem was "the place that I have chosen to set my name" (Nehemiah 1:9).

(Opposite page) The moon over the wall in Old City Jerusalem. Nehemiah wrote, "And I arose in the night, I and some few men with me . . . and viewed the walls of Jerusalem which were broken down" (Nehemiah 2:12-13).

FROM THE ORSON HYDE MEMORIAL GARDEN, you can see the walls of the Old City. I cannot look upon those walls without thinking of the dedication of Nehemiah and those who worked with him. After several decades of captivity in Babylon, the Persians allowed the Jews to return to rebuild their temple and city. Nehemiah was in a position of authority close to the king. Hearing that the walls of the city were still lying desolate, he petitioned the king for permission to return to Jerusalem and rebuild them. From our vantage point on the Mt. of Olives, we can picture Nehemiah rising in the darkness of the night to circle the city and survey the destroyed walls. Gathering the people the next day he announced, "Let us rise up and build. So they strengthened their hands for this good work" (Nehemiah 2:18).

One of my favorite chapters in the Old Testament is the third chapter of Nehemiah. I love to read it while examining the many stones in the walls of Jerusalem. Though I know these are not the original stones placed by Nehemiah and his workers, the wall on the eastern edge of the city lies in the same position. I can close my eyes, hear the ring of hammer on stone, and see the laboring men and women. The third chapter of Nehemiah lists the names of the workers who labored to build the wall. Here worked the family of "Shallum . . . and his daughters." Over there labored the "men of Jericho." Further down the wall the "goldsmiths" worked side by side with "the apothecaries." "Priests, . . . merchants, . . . and rulers" united in the common effort. They came from various cities, occupations, and families. Together, working side by side, facing tremendous opposition from their enemies, and inspired by the determined devotion of Nehemiah, they built the wall and set up its gates. Nehemiah honored them by mentioning each one by name and the place where they labored. "So we built the wall," he wrote, "for the people had a mind to work" (Nehemiah 4:6).

There is a unique and sacred feeling to the walls of Jerusalem. They were sanctified long ago by the efforts of many common people working together. I often wonder how they felt when the wall was completed and each individual could look at the stones he had helped set in place. Surely they came to the same conclusion as did Nehemiah and the enemies who mocked their efforts. "They perceived that this work was wrought of our God" (Nehemiah 6:16).

Perhaps this wonderful story was included in the Old Testament as an example for us today as we attempt to build the New

Jerusalem, the Zion of the latter day. Are we not also returning from the captivity of a spiritual Babylon? Should we not also have "a mind to work?" Do we not also need to strengthen our hands for this good work? Will not the durability of the wall we build today be determined by many thousands of common people laboring side by side in their respective wards and stakes? We all have an assignment at the wall. We each have our own stones to set in place, and the wall will be no stronger than the efforts of the least of its laborers. As I run my hands over the stones of Jerusalem's walls and reflect on the names Nehemiah chose to honor, I seem to see another list of names, recorded in the manuscripts of heaven by a loving Savior who recognizes and rewards each of us who labor for His kingdom. May we place our stones wisely and well as we labor side by side. Then, one day, all who view our work will "perceive that [it] was wrought of our God."

Then Nehemiah said, "Let us rise up and build. So they strengthened their hands for this good work" (Neh. 2:18). When his enemies tried to distract him from this task, Nehemiah replied "I am doing a great work, so that I cannot come down: why should the work cease, whilst I leave it, and come down to you?" (Neh. 6:3)

Follow the Prophets

When I was a little boy, I loved the story of Elijah being fed by the ravens. I thought it would be a wonderful thing to have birds bring you bread every morning and evening. Elijah was hiding by a brook in the land of Gilead, which is in the country of Jordan today. The first time I came to the Holy Land, we stopped in the Jordan River Valley, where I saw some large black and greyish birds. I asked our guide what species of birds were walking by the river. When he said they were ravens, a surprising flood of emotion washed over me. The imagination of my childhood returned, and the reality of the scriptures struck home. "These stories really did happen!" I thought.

The Jordan River.

Inset: Elijah receives food from the ravens.

THIS WAS THE FIRST of many similar moments where the land testified to the truthfulness of all I had believed from my childhood. Elijah seems to represent for me the essence of the Old Testament prophets—witnesses of the love our Father in Heaven has for His children, for they are one of the great gifts He bestows upon us. "And the Lord God of their fathers sent to them by his messengers, rising up betimes, and sending; because he had compassion on his people" (2 Chronicles 36:15).

I thought of that compassion from our vantage point on top of Mt. Carmel. Here Elijah made his stand against Jezebel's priests of Baal. With "all Israel" gathered to watch the contest, Elijah said to the people, "How long halt ye between two opinions? if the Lord be God, follow him: but if Baal, then follow him" (1 Kings 18:21).

The priests of Baal and then Elijah were to offer sacrifices to their respective gods, "and the God that answereth by fire, let him be God" (1 Kings 18:24). Walking among the stones of Mt. Carmel, one can almost feel the tension and excitement as the contest of gods took place. All morning and afternoon Baal's priests cried for the fire that would prove his existence, while Elijah mocked their efforts. "And there was neither voice, nor any to answer, nor any that regarded" (1 Kings 18:29).

In the fading light of the evening, Elijah prepared the offering. Then, to demonstrate the power of Jehovah, he poured barrel after barrel of water upon the wood and filled a trench that encircled the altar. As the sun sets over the Mediterranean, I can imagine the silhouette of Elijah as he kneels in prayer. "Lord God of Abraham, Isaac, and of Israel, let it be known this day that thou art God in Israel, and that I am thy servant, . . . Hear me, O Lord, hear me, that this people may know . . . that thou hast turned their heart back again" (1 Kings 18:36-37).

They were words that expressed the deepest desire of prophets, and the Lord responded by giving the asked-for fire from heaven, which "consumed the burnt sacrifice, and the wood, and the stones, and the dust, and licked up the water that was in the trench" (1 Kings 18:38).

The view from Mt. Carmel is beautiful. To the west lies the Mediterranean Sea and to the east the fertile Jezreel Valley. "Why do we not have such great prophetic manifestations today?" someone asked me. As I pondered the question, I knew that God has not changed.

He still answers by fire, the fire of the Holy Ghost. When we "halt between two opinions," latter-day prophets, like Elijah of old, continue to call down fire from heaven. I knew as I descended Mt. Carmel that I had been there many, many times before. I too had seen fire fall from a Father eager to show His children the way they should go.

A short drive brings us to the ancient site of Jezreel. Elijah ran this distance ahead of King Ahab after the confrontation at Carmel. Here stood Jezebel's palace and, close by, the vineyards of Naboth. Though prophets are a great benefit to man, they are so often misunderstood. Gazing at the vineyards of Jezreel, I think of Naboth who refused to sell them to Ahab and was conveniently stoned by Jezebel for it. With Naboth dead, Ahab walked in the vineyard savoring his new possession. Elijah met him there. But Ahab was not happy, and greeted him with the following words, "Hast thou found me, O mine enemy?" (1 Kings 21:20). I thought of the propensity of man to fight the guiding influence of prophets and thus cut themselves off from all the good they could receive. The concluding words of 2nd Chronicles come to mind, and I read them near the meeting place of Ahab and Elijah. "They mocked the messengers of God, and despised his words, and misused his prophets . . . till there was no remedy" (2 Chronicles 36:16).

(Above) Depiction of the test of Baal's prophets. In answering their challenge, the prophet Elijah said, "Call ye on the name of your gods, and I will call on the name of the Lord: and the God that answereth by fire, let him be God" (1 Kings 18:24).

(Left) Elijah's Monastery on Mt. Carmel. Elisha also frequented Mt. Carmel. On its slopes, a grieving mother pleaded with Elisha to return with her to Shunem and raise her only son from the dead. (See 2 Kings 4:18-37.)

(Opposite page) Statuette of God Baal, Beirut Museum.

NOT FAR FROM JEZREEL, I sit on the bank of the Jordan River and think of another man who questioned the wisdom and goodness of a prophet. Somewhere near here, Naaman, the Syrian captain, came at the instruction of Elisha to bathe seven times in the river. He was a leper, but the faith of a captive girl from Israel caused him to seek help from a prophet. Like so many of us, however, Naaman had his own ideas of what he wanted the prophet to say. "Are not Abana and Pharpar, rivers of Damascus, better than all the waters of Israel? Might I not wash in them, and be clean?" (2 Kings 5:12). Too often, we try to substitute our own ideas, programs, and plans for those given to us by the Lord through His prophets.

"If the prophet had bid thee do some great thing," his servants asked him, "wouldest thou not have done it? how much rather then, when he saith to thee, Wash, and be clean?" (2 Kings 5:13). Humbled by these words, Naaman "dipped himself seven times in Jordan, according to the saying of the man of God: and his flesh came again like unto the flesh of a little child" (2 Kings 5:14).

I wash my own hands in the Jordan while reflecting on Naaman. Washing is such a simple act. I wonder why he had instructed him to dip seven times in the river. Why not only once? Perhaps, if Naaman could speak today, he would answer, "It is the accumulation of many repeated and simple acts that brings the desired blessings. That is the way of prophets."

(Below) The Jordan River near the Sea of Galilee. Prophets not only respond to the great affairs of the Lord's kingdom, but are also sympathetic to the everyday cares of the people. Elisha made iron "swim" in the Jordan to retrieve a lost axe, thus relieving the anxiety of one of his followers who had borrowed it and lost it in the river. (See 2 Kings 6:5-7.)

(Opposite page) Dothan hill. The King of Syria sent his troops to Dothan to prevent Elisha from counseling the king of Israel. Elisha comforted his distraught servant with these words, "Fear not: for they that be with us are more than they that be with them" (2 Kings 6:16).

IN THE HILLS AND FIELDS OF NORTHERN SAMARIA lies Dothan. Once, jealous brothers sold Joseph into slavery from this place, but it is for another reason we have come to visit. I associate it more with hope than with Joseph's despairing cries. Here lived Elisha with his servant. Awakening one morning, the servant saw an army, complete with chariots, surrounding the city. They had been sent by the Syrian king to capture Elisha. Full of fear, the servant said, "Alas my master! How shall we do?" (2 Kings 6:15).

A prophet's eyes see more than ours do. Are they not also called See-ers? I try to imagine the wonder that must have entered the servant's heart as Elisha prayed. "Lord, . . . Open his eyes, that he may see . . . and he saw: and, behold, the mountain was full of horses and chariots of fire round about Elisha" (2 Kings 6:17). If we learn to trust prophetic vision, we may remain as calm as Elisha even in the midst of great opposition, for we will know, as they assure us, that the Lord watches over those who serve and love Him. In the trying times in which we live, where we are surrounded by the temptations and moral deterioration of modern society, the message we receive from the hills of Dothan brings comfort and hope.

I HAVE FELT THE CALM ASSURANCES of Dothan in Jerusalem while staring down the dark tunnel dug by Hezekiah's men in the fearful days of Assyrian domination. To secure his water supply, Hezekiah diverted the flow of the Gihon spring to the pool of Siloam. A favorite adventure in Jerusalem is to wade down the tunnel, flashlight in hand, while thinking of the courage of Hezekiah and his faith in the prophet Isaiah.

Though no nation had been able to stand against the might of Assyria, Isaiah promised that God would deliver His people if they would turn to Him. Believing in the words of his prophet, Hezekiah reformed his people, directed their attention to the temple, and taught them the commandments of the law. These were even more important preparations for the coming crisis than the marvelous feat of digging his famous tunnel. The northern ten tribes had just been taken captive when the Assyrian king sent a messenger to Hezekiah's people. "Let not Hezekiah deceive you, nor persuade you on this manner, neither yet believe him: for no god of any nation or kingdom was able to deliver his people out of mine hand . . . how much less shall your God deliver you?" (2 Chronicles 32:15).

Needing assurances to his faith, now that the crisis had arrived, Hezekiah sent messengers to Isaiah, asking him to pray for the people. Isaiah sent back the reassuring comfort of faith. "Be not afraid of the words that thou

(Above) Hezekiah's tunnel. Hezekiah made a pool and a conduit to secure a water source during the invasion of the Assyrians. The description of this amazing engineering feat is found in an inscription in the tunnel itself. "And this was the way in which it was cut through: each man [worked] toward his fellow, and while there were still three cubits to be cut through, [there was heard] the voice of a man calling to his fellow, for there was an overlap (or: fissure) in the rock on the right and on the left. And when the tunnel was driven through, the quarrymen hewed (the rock), each man toward his fellow, axe against axe, and the water flowed from the spring toward the reservoir for 1,200 cubits, and the height of the rock above the head(s) of the quarrymen was 100 cubits."

Trusting more in the Lord than in his tunnel, Hezekiah told his people, "Be strong and courageous, be not afraid nor dismayed for the king of Assyria, nor for all the multitude that is with him for there be more with us than with him; With him is an arm of flesh; but with us is the Lord our God" (2 Chron. 32:7-8).

(Opposite page) Pool of Siloam at the end of Hezekiahs tunnel. (Vignette) Assyrian arrowhead, possibly 2700 years old.

hast heard, . . . The king of Assyria . . . shall not come into this city, nor shoot an arrow there" (Isaiah 37:6, 33). A plague struck the Assyrian camp, and "Sennacherib king of Assyria departed" (Isaiah 37:37).

In the Old City of Jerusalem you can still see a section of the wall Hezekiah built during the Assyrian attack. Nearby I found a shop that sells antiquities. There in a tray with old coins and oil lamps lay the rusted remains of several arrow points. "How old is this arrowhead?" I asked, holding one up. "It's Assyrian," he answered, "twenty-seven hundred years old, but it was not found here in Jerusalem."

I thought of Isaiah's promise to Hezekiah, pooled all my resources, and bought the rusted point of metal. It rests in a prominent place in our home—a constant reminder of the blessings we may receive when we follow and trust the words of the Lord's prophets. When I touch it, I feel confident that if my family will follow the counsels of today's prophets, none of the fiery darts of the adversary will strike a fatal blow to those I love.

Looking out at the Mediterranean Sea from Joppa. Tel Aviv is in the distance. From beneath the waters of the Mediterranean Sea "Jonah prayed unto the Lord his God out of the fish's belly, and said, I cried by reason of mine affliction unto the Lord, and he heard me; out of the belly of hell cried I, and thou heardest my voice" (Jonah 2:1-2).

(Inset) Tel Nineveh the ancient capital of Assyria.

At Joppa, I think of the Assyrians in a different light, and the mercy of God is once again shown in the pages of the Old Testament. Here Jonah stood waiting for his ship to depart for the west. He had been called by the Lord to preach repentance in the streets of the Assyrian capital of Nineveh which lay to the east, but fear and animosity for his enemies overwhelmed him and he was fleeing. Though their wickedness was great, the Lord loved the Assyrians. Were they not His children also? Perhaps the power of a prophetic voice could turn them to repentance. The Lord's prophets speak not only to Israel, but to the whole world.

Three nights "in the belly of the fish," brought a change of heart to Jonah and he traveled to the city of his enemies and preached with all the powers of a prophet. His words were heeded, the people repented, and the city was spared. Though Jonah was at first displeased because the Lord was "a gracious God, and merciful, slow to anger, and of great kindness," (Jonah 4:2) in time he understood his Maker's heart.

"Should I not spare Nineveh, that great city," he asked Jonah, "wherein are more than sixscore thousand persons that cannot discern between their right hand and their left?" (Jonah 4:11). Staring out at the sea, the message of the tiny book of Jonah becomes crystal clear in my life. Cities all over the world, many of whose inhabitants do not know right from wrong, need the voice of prophets to guide them. If just two more young men, or one more older couple, decide to fill a mission instead of fleeing to the west as did Jonah, a whole city could be opened to the preaching of the gospel. How many more cities could hear and read the words of prophets, both living and dead, if just one more young person in every ward of the Church departed for the Ninevehs of the world, in spite of their fears?

Here at Joppa, one can hear Jonah's testimony whispering on the breezes of the Mediterranean. "You must not take the road of the sea as I did. You must not flee westward, but turn east to the waiting Ninevehs and teach them of their Savior's mercy and kindness."

FEAR OR FAITH

Tel Dan lies in the extreme northern part of the Holy Land. The headwaters of the Jordan are cold and refreshing as they run rapidly toward the Sea of Galilee. Under a large oak that shades one corner of Jeroboam's High Place, we read of a decision that marked the future path of the Ten Tribes of Israel. Life seems to turn on tiny hinges, and this place reinforces that truth in my mind.

At the death of Solomon, Jeroboam was promised by the prophet Ahijah that he and his posterity could rule the ten northern tribes of Israel. He was also promised "all that thy soul desireth" (1 Kings 11:37). He had to remain true to Jehovah and keep the commandments, however. When the tribes split, the tribe of Judah remained faithful to Rehoboam, the son of Solomon. Fearful that his people would turn to Rehoboam, because his territory contained the temple, Jeroboam made a decision of fear instead of faith. He built two golden calves, proclaimed them the gods of Israel, and erected them in Bethel and Dan.

Here at Tel Dan one can walk the very paving stones where the golden gods stood. I sense a deep sorrow as I walk these stones. Had Jeroboam but believed the prophet's promise, the whole history of Israel would have been different. As a result of this abandonment of Jehovah, the majority of the priesthood and righteous believers fled the northern kingdom and resettled in Judah to the south. Jeroboam's worst fears were realized, but ironically his own decision caused the flight.

The northern kingdom never recovered from this drain of the righteous, nor were the golden calves ever removed in later generations. They became the main gods of the ten tribes until the accumulation of their sins brought the Assyrian destruction that resulted in their becoming the Lost Ten Tribes. The beginning of that lost state can be dated from the day when Jeroboam placed a golden calf on the high place of Dan.

Waterfall near Mt. Hermon. Springs flowing from the melting snows of Mt. Hermon are the source of the Jordan. It flows to the Sea of Galilee, then follows a twisting route of 66 miles, where it enters the Dead Sea near Jericho. It varies in depth from 3 feet to 12 feet.

(Opposite page) Tel Dan, head waters of the Jordan River, and aerial view of Tel Dan. In Jeremiah, the Lord compared himself to a fountain of pure water and wondered why man refused to drink from its refreshing depths. "For my people have committed two evils; they have forsaken me the fountain of living waters, and hewed them out cisterns, broken cisterns, that can hold no water" (Jeremiah 2:13). The Lord makes a similar comparison when he asked, "Will a man leave the snow of Lebanon which cometh from the rock . . .?" (Jeremiah 18:14).

(Above) Elijah ascends into heaven. "Behold, there appeared a chariot of fire, and horses of fire; . . . And Elisha . . . cried, My father, my father, the chariot of Israel, and the horsemen thereof. And he saw him no more" (2 Kings 2:11-12).

WE LEAVE JOPPA TRAVELING EASTWARD toward Jerusalem, then down to Jericho and the Jordan River. Joshua split the Jordan here, thus allowing the children of Israel to cross on dry land just as Moses did with the Red Sea. Here, too, came Elijah and Elisha, walking together. Both men knew the time for Elijah's release was at hand. At Bethel and then again at Jericho, Elijah tried to get his companion to leave him, but Elisha would follow his master to the end. Arriving at the river, Elijah "took his mantle, and wrapped it together, and smote the waters, and they were divided hither and thither, so that they two went over on dry ground" (2 Kings 2:8). As they walked, a chariot of fire appeared, parting them, "and Elijah went up by a whirlwind into heaven" (2 Kings 2:11).

Though Elijah was gone, the Lord did not leave His people without the guidance of a prophet. In a symbolic gesture, He let Elijah's mantle fall back to the ground. " Walking to the Jordan River, "Elisha took the mantle of Elijah . . . and smote the waters, and said, Where is the Lord God of Elijah? and when he also had smitten the waters, they parted hither and thither: and Elisha went over" (2 Kings 2:13-14).

Those watching drew the right conclusion from the physical manifestation of a spiritual reality. "When the sons of the prophets . . . saw him, they said, The spirit of Elijah doth rest on Elisha" (2 Kings 2:15). Here by the Jordan, we too would be "sons of the prophets," a phrase which means we follow their teachings and share their faith. The mantle still falls upon the President of the Church. I listened one evening to President Gordon B. Hinckley as he spoke in the chapel of the Jerusalem Center. The Old City provided the backdrop as the mantle of all the Old Testament prophets descended upon him. If I could have heard the voices of Moses, or Isaiah, or Elijah, I knew in that moment that their voices would not have been more powerful than the voice to which I was listening. There is one message the Old Testament forcefully imparts on almost every page. In this holy land of the prophets, site after site testifies to the truth so beautifully stated by Amos: "Surely the Lord God will do nothing, but he revealeth his secret unto his servants the prophets" (Amos 3:7).

WATCHMEN ON THE TOWER

Watchtowers are scattered throughout the Holy Land—on isolated hills, or brooding over the busy streets of Jerusalem. Some are in ruins, but the view from their summit always commands a wide area. I often turn to the Lord's words to Ezekiel when surveying the broad vista spread below. The role of a prophet was to be "a watchman unto the house of Israel . . . (Ezekiel 3:17). The Lord's metaphor seems clear from this vantage point above the city: when a prophet speaks, we should always ask, "I wonder what he sees that has caused him to deliver to us his counsel." If one learns to trust the watchman's wider vision, and take warning from his sight, Ezekiel promises "he shall . . . deliver his soul" (Ezekiel 33:5).

Old watchtower in a field. Using the image of a watchman on the tower, Joseph Smith wrote, "The watchman on the tower would have seen the enemy while he was yet afar off; and then ye could have made ready . . ." (D&C 101:54).

VISION OF SEERS

When I was little, I dreamed of digging up buried treasure; and those old emotions always stir within me when visiting the Shrine of the Book in Jerusalem. In the caves around the Dead Sea, the greatest treasure ever found in the Middle East was discovered. That treasure consisted of scrolls covering every book of the Old Testament except Esther. I feel a boyhood tingle of excitement as I stare through the glass at the Isaiah scroll. It is fitting that the Holy Land's treasures are these scrolls—not golden artifacts of ancient kings, but written words of holy prophets.

The Shrine of the Book.   Inset: Ancient scrolls.

"HE THAT IS NOW CALLED A PROPHET, was beforetime called a Seer" (1 Samuel 9:9). What inspiring truths they saw and revealed to us. Drawing upon the scenery and objects around them, the Old Testament seers inspired and lifted generations, as they continue to lift us now. One cannot travel anywhere in the Holy Land without being reminded of the wonderful insights of Isaiah, Ezekiel, Hosea, Micah, and others.

The descent from Jerusalem to Jericho passes through the dry Judean Wilderness. It is hard to imagine a harsher climate, but even here there is water. Water means life in this land. Nephi, who knew this country, revealed that "the fountain of living waters . . . are a representation of the love of God" (1 Nephi 1:25). I think of this distinction as I read the words of the prophets. "When the poor and needy seek water, and there is none, and their tongue faileth for thirst, I the Lord will hear them, I the God of Israel will not forsake them. I will open rivers in high places, and fountains in the midst of the valleys: I will make the wilderness a pool of water, and the dry land springs of water" (Isaiah 41:17-18). In a dry world where abiding love is so often lacking, the Savior cries, "Ho, every one that thirsteth, come ye to the waters, and he that hath no money; come ye, buy, and eat; yea, come, buy wine and milk without money and without price" (Isaiah 55:1).

In the reeds by the river's edge, other promises of Isaiah ring true in my ears. "I will pour water upon him that is thirsty, and floods upon the dry ground: I will pour my spirit upon thy seed, and my blessing upon thine offspring: And they shall spring up as among the grass, as willows by the water courses" (Isaiah 44:3-4). I read those words one year and lifted my eyes to watch my son, walking along the water's edge. A flood of gratitude swept through me, for I knew the Lord would keep His promises. Isaiah was as vital to me that day as he was to anyone in any past generation.

I will make the wilderness a pool of water, and the dry land springs of water.

(Opposite page) Isaiah in prayer.

(Opposite page) Reeds in the Sea of Galilee at sunrise.

(Above) Fragment of scroll found at Qumran, where the Dead Sea Scrolls were found.

(Left) Wadi Qelt, Judean Desert near Jericho. This riverbed descends from Jericho and goes from the Dead Sea toward Jerusalem. "It was a river that I could not pass over: for the waters were risen . . . now when I had returned, behold, at the bank of the river were very many trees on the one side and on the other" (Ezekiel 47:5, 7). John used this image also in describing the center of God's eternal kingdom in Revelation 22.

THE DEAD SEA

Sodom and Gomorrah once stood in the vicinity of the Dead Sea. Here, Lot "pitched his tent toward Sodom" (Gen. 13:12). His choice to approach too closely to the world had tragic consequences for his family. Some members died in the destruction of Sodom, including his wife. The behavior of Lot's daughters later indicates that the morals of Sodom had affected even them. We must be careful our own tents do not face the alluring world of modern Sodom. The salt pillars remind me of Lot's wife who was warned not to even look back. When we leave the "world," we must leave for good. There is danger in that last lingering backward glance. Often, old lifestyles pull at us and we may not have the strength to remain free of its influences. In a modern revelation, the Lord counsels, "Go ye out . . . from the midst of wickedness, which is spiritual Babylon. . . . And he that goeth, let him not look back lest sudden destruction shall come upon him" (D&C 133:14-15). Yet even in this barren waste of salt and desert, I am reminded of the Lord's mercy and that of his prophets. Did not Abraham plead with the Lord to spare the cities of Sodom and Gomhorrah if he could find just ten righteous souls? Perhaps if Lot's family had held a truer course of integrity, the ten righteous souls would have been found. Our own responsibility becomes plain. We must be part of the ten righteous souls in our own cities and nations that the Lord is longing to behold.

The barren shore of the Dead Sea. In 1947, the Dead Sea Scrolls were discovered by goatherders in Qumran, near the northwest corner of the Dead Sea. The contents of these scrolls attest to the intellectual and literary integrity of those who wrote and preserved their records. Their historical and textual content constitute one of the most important archaeological discoveries of modern times. (See Bible Dictionary.)

IT WOULD BE HARD FOR ME TO CHOOSE one Old Testament site in this land that touches me more than any other, yet there is one I never fail to visit. It is an overlook midway between Jerusalem and Jericho, from which one can see the open barrenness of the Wilderness reaching up to Jerusalem on the west, and down to the Dead Sea on the east. From here, I can picture the fulfillment of Ezekiel's wonderful prophecy and the rivers that will one day flow through this dead land.

Ezekiel saw in vision a temple constructed in Jerusalem. From the threshold of the temple a spring of water issues forth and begins to flow eastward. It descends through the wilderness and empties into the Dead Sea. Everywhere the river flows, life springs up on its banks. Ezekiel saw "very many trees on the one side and on the other" (Ezekiel 47:7). When the water reaches the Dead Sea, "the waters shall be healed. And it shall come to pass, that everything that liveth, which moveth, whithersoever the rivers shall come, shall live: and there shall be a very great multitude of fish, because these waters shall come hither: for they shall be healed; and every thing shall live whither the river cometh" (Ezekiel 47:8-9). Ezekiel then saw fishermen dividing their catch and drying their nets on the shores of the Dead Sea.

How can anything bring these dead places to bountiful life? As I feel the heat of the desert and gaze at the salt shores of the Dead Sea, the power of the Lord's love and light as they flow from His temples sinks deep into my heart. As Ezekiel walked down the length of the river, he was instructed to wade into its cooling freshness. With each new entrance the waters are deeper, until they become, "waters to swim in." I suppose there really is no bottom to the river of our Savior's love.

(Above) Two Ibex at the En-gedi Reserve. The prophets of the Old Testament often used animals to teach their vital lessons. It was also said of Solomon's wisdom that "he spake of beasts, and of fowl, and of creeping things, and of fishes" (1 Kings 4:33). All things are part of our Father in Heaven's great schoolroom of mortality.

Every prophet of the Old Testament spoke of the mercy, kindness, and compassion of their God. I think they would be puzzled by our modern difficulty with the God of the Old Testament. He is so often spoken of today as a God of justice and vengeance. I have heard people ask how the Jehovah of the Old Testament can be the same Jesus of the New Testament. I sense that the prophets would be mystified by our evaluation. "Listen to our words and look upon our world!" they would tell us.

If we turned at their bidding and looked at the hills and mountains of Israel, we would hear Isaiah's gentle words, "For the mountains shall depart, and the hills be removed; but my kindness shall not depart from thee, neither shall the covenant of my peace be removed, saith the Lord that hath mercy on thee" (Isaiah 54:10).

Jeremiah used the metaphor of thirst and fatigue to describe the Lord's goodness. "My people shall be satisfied with my goodness, . . . For I have satiated the weary soul, and I have replenished every sorrowful soul" (Jeremiah 31:14, 25). Hosea drew upon the joy of courtship and marriage, writing, "I will betroth thee unto me for ever; yea, I will betroth thee unto me in righteousness, and in judgement, and in lovingkindness, and in mercies. I will even betroth thee unto me in faithfulness" (Hosea 2:19-20). Joel encouraged his people to "turn unto the Lord your God: for he is gracious and merciful, slow to anger, and of great kindness" (Joel 2:13).

Staring down into the depths of the sea, I am reminded of Micah's testimony of how willing Jehovah is to forgive. "Who is a God like unto thee, that pardoneth iniquity, . . . he delighteth in mercy. . . . he will have compassion upon us . . . and thou wilt cast all their sins into the depths of the sea" (Micah 7:18-19). While looking at the strong towers of Jerusalem, Nahum's comparison becomes a reality. "The Lord is good, a strong hold in the day of trouble; and he knoweth them that trust in him" (Nahum 1:7). The words of Habakkuk ring true while we watch the sure-footed ibex climbing the perpendicular cliffs at En-gedi. "The Lord God is my strength, and he will make my feet like hinds' feet, and he will make me to walk upon mine high places" (Habakkuk 3:19).

INCLINE THINE EAR UNTO WISDOM

The writers of the Old Testament were not afraid to tackle the great moral and philosophical questions that have troubled and perplexed man from the beginning. The problem of human suffering is deeply explored by Job. Habakkuk pondered the apparent triumph of evil over good, asking the Lord, "How long shall I cry, and thou wilt not hear! . . . Why dost thou shew me iniquity and cause me to behold grievance? . . . judgement doth never go forth: for the wicked doth compass about the righteous" (Habakkuk 1:2-4). The people in Malachi's day wondered if it was "vain to serve God," because "we call the proud happy; yea, they that work wickedness are set up" (Malachi 3:14-15).

"In an uncertain world, what is the best and the happiest life to live?" asks the Book of Ecclesiastes. Since "all is vanity," can fulfillment ever be realized? Is it found in wealth and comfort? Fame? Learning and wisdom? Long life? Pleasure? Youth? New and ever-changing experiences? Is it discovered in simple labor, family love, and obedience? The Lord's answers to all these questions can be discovered in the Old Testament.

(Left) Arabian men deep in discussion at the sheep market by the Old City Wall in Jerusalem, Israel.

*I will feed my flock ...
I will seek that
which was lost.*

(Above) Ezekiel prophesying, "Now it came to pass ... that the heavens were opened, and I saw visions of God" (Ezekiel 1:1).

(Left) Shepherd sits with his flock, just as Christ watches constantly over us.

(Opposite page) Fishing boat on the Sea of Galilee.

L ISTENING TO THE JOYFUL VOICES of singing children reminds us that Zephaniah once used that glad sound to speak of his God. "The Lord thy God in the midst of thee is mighty; he will save, he will rejoice over thee with joy; he will rest in his love, he will joy over thee with singing" (Zephaniah 3:17). Haggai described God as "the desire of all nations" (Haggai 2:7). Zechariah affirmed, "How great is his goodness, and how great is his beauty!" (Zechariah 9:17). Malachi knew God desired to "open the windows of heaven, and pour you out a blessing, that there shall not be room enough to receive it" (Malachi 3:10). Every way they could, using every object or part of nature, the prophets taught of God's overwhelming goodness.

The most fitting image the ancient seers chose for their God was that of a devoted shepherd. "The Lord is my shepherd," David wrote, "I shall not want . . ." (Psalms 23:1). That beautiful image was magnified by Ezekiel's description, "I will feed my flock, and I will cause them to lie down . . . I will seek that which was lost, and bring again that which was driven away, and will bind up that which was broken, and will strengthen that which was sick" (Ezekiel 34:15-16). Isaiah knew his God would "feed his flock like a shepherd: he shall gather the lambs with his arm, and carry them in his bosom" (Isaiah 40:11).

The vision of these prophets did not limit itself to their own day. Their testimony of the kindness of Jehovah was strengthened by their understanding of the latter-day fulfillment of all they longed to see. How they thrilled while viewing the marvelous work and wonder of the Restoration. I am reminded of this in Galilee while watching the fishermen casting their nets. Scattered Israel is being gathered by Jeremiah's fishers and hunters. "I will send for many fishers, saith the Lord, and they shall fish them; and after will I send for many hunters, and they shall hunt them from every mountain, and from every hill, and out of the holes of the rocks" (Jeremiah 16:16). The fisherman draws his nets to shore filled with fish. I think of my sons and daughter serving in the mission field. Some were like this fisherman; they cast the gospel net and baptized many souls. One was called to be a hunter and spent her mission looking for the one or two still hiding in the rocks. Both fishers and hunters are necessary.

STANDING IN THE STREETS OF JERUSALEM one afternoon, I think of the Restoration with its key element, the Book of Mormon. On the pavement before me sits a blind beggar. Though he held his hand out for coins, I knew that if he could have his greatest desire it would be the restoration of his sight. Isaiah was aware of the spiritual blindness of the latter-day world. He also knew the Lord would bring out of the ground a book that would grant sight to any who desired it. "And in that day," he wrote, "shall the deaf hear the words of the book, and the eyes of the blind shall see out of obscurity, and out of darkness" (Isaiah 29:18). Yet how many today want only a few tossed coins rather than the light of eternity? Ezekiel, too, wrote of the Book of Mormon, adding the insight that it would be joined with the Bible to accomplish the Lord's work. The "stick of Joseph" and the "stick of Judah . . . shall become one in thine hand" (Ezekiel 37:16-17).

Almost every aspect of the Restoration was seen by the seers of old. Perhaps that is why Moroni turned to the Old Testament when he visited Joseph Smith in the upper room of the Smith cabin in 1823, drawing upon words three thousand years old to teach Joseph of his mission. Obadiah spoke of "saviors . . . on mount Zion" (Obadiah 1:28); and Malachi foretold of the coming of Elijah who would "turn the hearts of the fathers to the children, and the hearts of the children to their fathers" (Malachi 4:6). Joel prophesied

the Lord would "pour out [his] spirit upon all flesh; and your sons and your daughters shall prophesy, and your old men shall dream dreams, your young men shall see visions" (Joel 2:28). Amos wrote of the great spiritual famine that would cover the land, "not a famine of bread, nor a thirst for water, but of hearing the words of the Lord" (Amos 8:11). Micah promised that the Lord's saints would "be in the midst of many people as a dew from the Lord, as the showers upon the grass," which would bring life and cleansing (Micah 5:7). That verse's beauty deepens in my heart one evening when a gentle rain cools us from the heat of a dusty day. Daniel spoke of the rapid growth of the latter-day work, beginning as "a stone . . . cut out of the mountain," and ending with "a great mountain [which] filled the whole earth" (Daniel 2:35, 45).

These are but a few examples of the multitude of visions these seers had concerning our day. I used to read the stories of the Old Testament and wish I had lived in the days of the prophets to witness seas splitting, pillars of fire lighting the wilderness, giants being slain, and chariots ascending into heaven. I should have liked to gather the manna, the wonderful bread from heaven. In contemplating these miraculous works, I failed to realize the "marvelous work" of my own day.

When Jeremiah looked upon our generation and compared it to the wondrous works of the Old Testament, he said, "The days come . . . that they shall no more say, The

(Opposite page) Beggar sitting in the streets of Jerusalem. The Old Testament prophets showed great concern for the poor. Moses wrote, "If there be among you a poor man of one of thy brethren . . . thou shalt not . . . shut thine hand from thy poor brother; But thou shalt open thine hand wide unto him . . . and thine heart shall not be grieved when thou givest unto him: because . . . for this thing the Lord thy God shall bless thee in all thy works . . ." (Deut. 15:7-8, 10-11). Isaiah, too, records the Lord's admonition for caring for the needy. "Is not this the fast that I have chosen? . . . to undo the heavy burdens . . . to deal thy bread to the hungry, and . . . when thou seest the naked, that thou cover him; . . ." (Isaiah 58:6-7).

the small RAIN

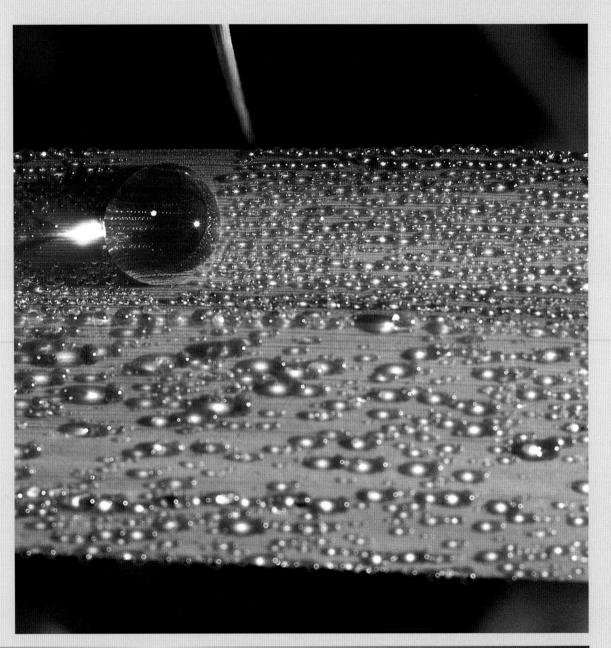

Spring showers in the Holy Land make the air sweet and clean and cover the hills with grass and wild flowers. Though the common perception that the laws and commandments of the Old Testament are harsh, the Lord Himself compared them to light rains and early morning dew. "My doctrine shall drop as the rain, my speech shall distill as the dew, as the small rain upon the tender herbs, and as the showers upon the grass" (Deuteronomy 32:2). The teachings of the Lord are not designed to restrict us, but to refresh, enliven, and cleanse.

Lord liveth, which brought up the children of Israel out of . . . Egypt; but, The Lord liveth, which brought up and which led the seed of the house of Israel out of the north country, and from all countries whither [he] had driven them . . ." (Jeremiah 23:7-8). The dispensation of the fulness of times was the age they all looked forward to. The gathering of Israel was, in their minds, more tremendous than the exodus from Egypt. The latter-day wonders would eclipse those of their own world. How much I take for granted that which they longed to see. In their world there was only one temple, and only a few could enter it. Isaiah must have been amazed to see the floods of Latter-day Saint men and women of all nations pouring into the many temples of our day; for the Lord revealed to him "the sons of the stranger . . . will I bring to my holy mountain, and make them joyful in my house of prayer . . . for mine house shall be called an house of prayer for all people" (Isaiah 56:7). Into that house of prayer "all nations shall flow" (Isaiah 2:2).

Though Old Testament prophets and seers were pained by the apostasy and scattering of their own generation, they were positive men of joy and hope. They knew, by experience, the perfect love of God. They saw the majesty of the day you and I are allowed to live in. They saw the eventual downfall of spiritual Babylon and the ultimate triumph of goodness. They saw the multitude of God's tender mercies showered upon His children, and wrote extensively of those gifts and that kindness. But above all things, they saw God's greatest manifestation of mercy—the life and mission of His Son.

(Above) While in prison, Jeremiah had Baruch record his prophecies. The King and his counsellors burned the writings, but Baruch rewrote all the former words as Jeremiah had dictated "and there were added besides unto them many like words" (Jer. 36:32).

(Left) Light shines heavenword from the Mt. of Beatitudes, symbolic of the light in God's holy temples. "And many will people shall . . . say, Come ye, and let us go up to the mountain of the Lord, to the house of the God of Jacob; and he will teach us his ways, . . ." (Isaiah 2:3).

MESSIAH

On the morning of the resurrection, Jesus appeared to two disciples while they traveled toward a village called Emmaus. Though they conversed with the Savior, their "eyes were holden that they should not know him" (Luke 24:16). This inability to recognize the Savior was not just physical. They were, also, to a large extent, unaware of His mission. Still holding to old traditions concerning their Messiah, they were confused by His death and rumors of His resurrection. To help them understand His true atoning mission, Jesus taught them out of the pages of the Old Testament. "Beginning at Moses and all the prophets, he expounded unto them in all the scriptures the things concerning himself" (Luke 24:27). Arriving at Emmaus, they invited Christ to abide with them. After breaking bread, "their eyes were opened, and they knew him; and he vanished out of their sight. And they said one to another, Did not our heart burn within us, while he talked with us by the way, and while he opened to us the scriptures?" (Luke 24:31=32).

The Sea of Galilee.   Inset: Christ appears to his disciples in Emmaus.

WHEN I WAS FIRST ASKED to write the text for this book, I was excited because I love the sites of the Holy Land associated with the Old Testament. Yet I also felt somewhat disappointed, because my memories of the Holy Land tied so closely to thoughts of Christ and the New Testament. However, the Savior Himself used the Old Testament to teach His disciples the true meaning of His life and mission, and in such a manner that their hearts burned within them. The ancient prophets foresaw His ministry, thus attaching importance to many places in the Holy Land before Jesus was ever born. With the Old Testament as our guide, the life of Christ unfolds before us. Many centuries before a star shone over Bethlehem, these ancient prophets foretold the paths the Savior would walk.

Perhaps Micah saw that star, the stable over which it shone, and the visit of the humble shepherds, for he wrote: "But thou, Bethlehem Ephratah, though thou be little among the thousands of Judah, yet out of thee shall he come forth unto me that is to be ruler in Israel; whose goings forth have been from of old, from everlasting" (Micah 5:2). Bethlehem is still a little place. Yet, as we bend to enter the Church of the Nativity, and sing Christmas carols in the grotto, we feel the assurance of Micah's testimony that the child that was laid in a manger here did in reality become "great unto the ends of the earth" (Micah 5:4). And as Isaiah said when viewing in vision the same miraculous birth, "For unto us a child is born . . . and his name shall be called Wonderful" (Isaiah 9:6).

The hills and valleys around Nazareth project a sacred feeling. As a boy and young man, Jesus walked this land. In solitary places He communed with His Father and learned of His mission. Though we know very little about the first thirty years of our Savior's life, perhaps Isaiah hinted at the intense schooling of those years when he wrote: "The Lord God hath given me the tongue of the learned, that I should know how to speak a word in season to him that is weary: he wakeneth morning by morning, he wakeneth mine ear to hear as the learned" (Isaiah 50:4). During His recorded ministry, the Savior continued the patterns of His youth, "rising up a great while before day" to search for "a solitary place, and there pray" (Mark 1:35).

In order for Jesus to understand our needs, He spent His first thirty years of life in the common pursuits we all engage in. He labored under Joseph's direction, laughed and played with brothers and sisters, and was "subject" to His mother. Isaiah described those years with a metaphor. "He shall grow up before him as a tender plant, and as a root out of a dry ground: he hath no form nor comeliness; and when we shall see him, there is no beauty that we should desire him." During those years He would become "acquainted with grief," that He might better "[bear] our griefs, and carry our sorrows" (Isaiah 53:2-4).

While standing on a promontory that looks out over the Judean Wilderness, I wonder if Isaiah gazed upon a similar scene when he heard the future "voice of him that crieth in the wilderness, Prepare ye the way of the Lord, make straight in the desert a highway for our God" (Isaiah 40:3). This wilderness is such a lonely, solitary place. Surely it molded the character of John the Baptist, making him strong in the Spirit and powerful in his message of repentance. And yet, the voice Isaiah heard was also a soft and inviting voice. "Comfort ye, comfort ye my people, saith your God. Speak ye comfortably to Jerusalem" (Isaiah 40:1-2). The "highway" John instructed the people to build was designed that the Lord might come quickly to His people and bring His comforting message of healing and hope.

To Isaiah, the Savior's comforting guidance of His people was likened to that of a shepherd. "He shall feed his flock . . . he shall gather the lambs with his arm, and carry them in his bosom, and shall gently lead those that are with young" (Isaiah 40:11).

This gentle influence would extend to the elements. All things became calm in the presence of the Great Creator. On the Sea of Galilee, Jesus twice calmed the waves and the wind. Did David see those moments, causing him to write,

With the Old Testament as our guide, the life of Christ unfolds before us.

They that go down to the sea in ships, . . . These see the works of the Lord . . . For he commandeth, and raiseth the stormy wind, which lifteth up the waves thereof. They mount up to the heaven, they go down again to the depths: their soul is melted because of trouble. They reel to and fro, and stagger like a drunken man, and are at their wits' end. Then they cry unto the Lord in their trouble, and he bringeth them out of their distresses. He maketh the storm a calm, so that the waves thereof are still. Then are they glad because they be quiet; so he bringeth them unto their desired haven (Psalms 107:23-30).

Early in His ministry, when Jesus wanted the people of His own village of Nazareth to understand Him, He relied on the prophetic words of the Old Testament to express what He had been called by His Father to do. How many of the events of the Savior's life are contained in these beautiful words? How often did Jesus read them during His formative years and ponder their fulfillment? "The Spirit of the Lord God is upon me; because the Lord hath anointed me to preach good tidings unto the meek; he hath sent me to bind up the brokenhearted, to proclaim liberty to the captives, and the opening of the prison to them that are bound" (Isaiah 61:1).

The Golden Gate in the east wall of the Old City of Jerusalem is sealed up now. It is the traditional gate through which Christ passed when He rode triumphant into Jerusalem on a donkey. Triumphs were given to Roman generals after they had won great victories. Standing before this gate two thou-

(Right) The Golden Gate is located in the east wall of the Old City of Jerusalem, and is sealed up now

(Inset below) This 14-point star is located in the marble floor in the grotto beneath the Church of the Nativity in Bethlehem. This is the alleged site of Jesus' birth. Here Isaiah's prophecy would be fulfilled that "a virgin shall conceive, and bear a son, and shall call his name Immanuel" (Isaiah 7:14).

sand years later, I think about the victories of Christ's life. For thirty-three years, as Paul stated, Christ "was in all points tempted like as we are, yet without sin" (Hebrews 4:15). That victory was worth more than all the Roman victories put together, yet He rode on a donkey—a sign of humility. Did He not also triumph over pride? He would also conquer sin and death for all of us. Did not the ringing words of "Hosanna" foreshadow that greatest of all triumphs?

Such a significant moment did not go unnoticed by those of old. Zechariah, struck by the beauty of Christ's humble entrance into Jerusalem penned the following words. "Rejoice greatly, O daughter of Zion; shout, O daughter of Jerusalem: behold, thy King cometh unto thee: he is just, and having salvation; lowly, and riding upon an ass, and upon a colt the foal of an ass" (Zechariah 9:9).

The highlight of every trip I have made to the Holy Land comes on the last day, when we retrace the footsteps of Jesus during the last hours of His life. Of all the events foreseen by the prophets, the atoning hours are described in the greatest detail. On this visit, I read only the Old Testament as we walk from site to site. To relive the last hours of Christ with the Old Testament is to share a unique and wonderful closeness with the Master, for so many of the scriptures we read express the thoughts and words of Christ Himself.

IN THE UPPER ROOM, the betrayal will culminate as Judas receives the "sop" from Jesus and walks into the darkness of the night. David's psalms reflect the feelings of the Savior at that moment. "Yea, mine own familiar friend, in whom I trusted, which did eat of my bread, hath lifted up his heel against me. . . . For it was not an enemy that reproached me; then I could have borne it: . . . But it was thou, a man mine equal, my guide, and mine acquaintance. We took sweet counsel together, and walked unto the house of God in company" (Psalms 41:9; 55:12-14).

Zechariah, also, was deeply moved by the sorrow of Christ's betrayal. He, too, gives us a glimpse into the soul of the Master. "And I said unto them, If ye think good, give me my price; and if not, forbear. So they weighed for my price thirty pieces of silver. . . . a goodly price that I was prized at of them" (Zechariah 11:12-13).

From the Upper Room it is a short walk down into the Kidron Valley to the Garden of Gethsemane. At the Last Supper, Jesus had asked His disciples to drink the sacrament cup in memorial of His coming sacrifice. Now it was time for Him to drink the cup His Father had given Him. We turn to the wisdom of Isaiah and read of Gethsemane and a bitter cup, which the Savior would take out of our hands. "Thus saith thy Lord the Lord, and thy God that pleadeth the cause of his people, Behold, I have taken out of thine hand the cup of trembling, even the dregs of the cup of my fury; thou shalt

no more drink it again" (Isaiah 51:22). With Isaiah's words in mind, we also read the prayer Jesus offered. "O my Father, if it be possible, let this cup pass from me: nevertheless not as I will, but as thou wilt" (Matthew 26:39).

The prophets knew of the atoning mercy of Jesus, and the price He would pay to offer forgiveness to all mankind. Through the pains of Gethsemane, Jesus cries out to us, "I . . . will not remember thy sins . . . I have blotted out, as a thick cloud, thy transgressions, and, as a cloud, thy sins: return unto me; for I have redeemed thee" (Isaiah 43:25; 44:22).

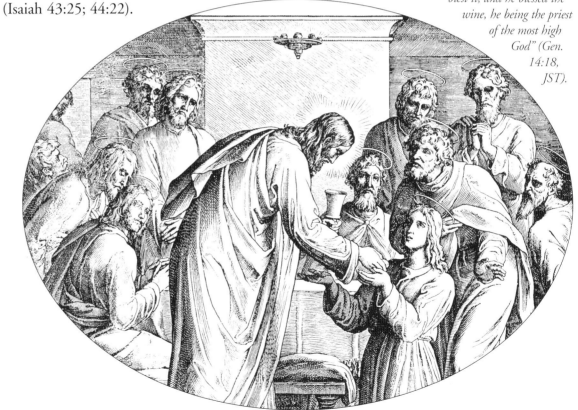

S THE AGONIES OF GETHSEMANE drained life and strength from Him, Jesus looked up to see the arresting party led by Judas. Earlier that night, at the entrance to Gethsemane, Jesus, familiar with the writings of Zechariah, told His disciples that they would leave Him. To their unbelieving ears, He reviewed what the prophet wrote centuries earlier. I will "smite the shepherd, and the sheep shall be scattered" (Zechariah 13:7). Peter drew his sword, but the Savior quieted him with the assurance that all that the prophets had foretold must be fulfilled. "Thinkest thou not that I cannot now pray to my Father," Jesus said, "and he shall presently give me more than twelve legions of angels? But how then shall the scriptures be fulfilled, that thus it must be? (Matthew 26:53-54).

Through years of study, Jesus knew what fulfilling the scriptures meant. I have often wondered what His thoughts were when, as a boy poring over the writings of Isaiah, He read of the mission of the Messiah and knew that Calvary lay ahead. Even before the ultimate mockery of Calvary, however, the trials and scourging awaited Him. He knew of these moments also and submitted Himself to the arresting party while His disciples fled.

We ascend the hill of Mt. Zion to the remains of Caiaphas's Palace, which are enshrined in the Church of St. Peter in Gallicantu. The Savior was brought here to face the high priest and members of the

Sanhedrin. The words of Isaiah contrast sharply with the peaceful reverence that pervades the church. As in so many other examples, Isaiah records the words as if Christ Himself were speaking. "The Lord God hath opened mine ear, and I was not rebellious, neither turned away back. I gave my back to the smiters, and my cheeks to them that plucked off the hair: I hid not my face from shame and spitting" (Isaiah 50:5-6).

These words stay in our minds while we walk across the old Roman paving stones where Pilate tried and failed to save Jesus, and where he delivered Him to be beaten and crucified. Pilate said, "I find in him no fault at all" (John 18:38). The prophets knew of His sinless state before Pilate gave this judgement, the truest verdict in history. "He had done no violence, neither was any deceit in his mouth" (Isaiah 53:9). While staring at the games the Roman soldiers scratched in the stone so many

centuries before, the words of Isaiah take on new relevance. "He was wounded for our transgressions, he was bruised for our iniquities: the chastisement of our peace was upon him; and with his stripes we are healed. . . . He was oppressed, and he was afflicted, yet he opened not his mouth" (Isaiah 53:5, 7).

Moved by the Savior's love and suffering we walk through the streets of the Old City, through the Damascus Gate toward Calvary, the place of the skull. "He was taken from prison and from judgment," echoes in our ears while we push through the ever-present crowds at the gate (Isaiah 53:8). So many details of Christ's agonies at this place were foreseen and recorded in the poetic rhythms and power of Old Testament prophecy. Such exquisite sacrifice must not be forgotten, and was remembered by Jehovah's prophets even before it was accomplished.

(Opposite page) 2,000-year-old steps that lead to the palace of Caiaphas.

(Above) The Damascus Gate, one of eight gates in Old City Jerusalem, is one of the most ornate.

(Left) The old Damascus gate below the level of the present city.

(Opposite page) The Garden Tomb. In the New Testament we witness the Atoning hours leading to the triumph of the resurrection through the eyes of the disciples; in the Old Testament we experience it through the thoughts and heart of Jesus himself.

CRUCIFIED BETWEEN SINNERS HE CAME TO SAVE, Christ "made his grave with the wicked . . . and was numbered with the transgressors" (Isaiah 53:9, 12). Though the New Testament accounts of the crucifixion are moving, nothing touches me more deeply than reading the Psalms here in the shadow of Calvary. They seem to express the heart of Christ, drawing me into His thoughts while He hung on the cross to pay the price of mortality. In the immense isolation of His loneliness and pain, He turned to the words of David and cried, "My God, My God, why hast thou forsaken me?" (Psalms 22:1). This is a time to be alone as our group separates to ponder and reflect. I turn back to David's insight and read the rest of his Psalm. His words create a window into the Savior's mind as He "poured out his soul unto death" (Isaiah 53:12).

"Why art thou so far from helping me, and from the words of my roaring," David wrote. "But I am a worm, and no man; a reproach of men, and despised of the people. All they that see me laugh me to scorn: they shoot out the lip, they shake the head, saying, He trusted on the Lord that he would deliver him: let him deliver him, seeing he delighted in him. . . . I am poured out like water, and all my bones are out of joint: my heart is like wax; . . . My strength is dried up like a potsherd; and my tongue cleaveth to my jaws; and thou hast brought me into the dust of death. . . . The wicked have inclosed me: they pierced my hands and my feet. . . . they look and stare upon me. They part my garments among them, and cast lots upon my vesture" (Psalms 22:1-18).

All these things, however, He could bear. The one thing that was most difficult was the necessary withdrawal of His Father that Christ might, on His own, complete the Atonement for sin. All His life He had felt the comforting presence of His Father in Heaven. Even at the Last Supper when He told the disciples that they would leave Him, He said, "Yet I am not alone, because the Father is with me" (John 16:12). On the cross, however, He would call out to that Father. "But thou art he that took me out of the womb; thou didst make me hope when I was upon my mother's breasts. I was cast upon thee from the womb . . . . Be not thou far from me, O Lord: O my strength, haste thee to help me" (Psalms 22:9-10, 19).

Toward the end, Jesus made one simple request. "I thirst." "And the soldiers also mocked him, coming to him, and offering him vinegar" (Luke 23:36). Even the soothing comfort of water to quench His thirst was denied. I turn to the sixty-ninth Psalm and read the words that draw me closer to the heart of Jesus during those last moments on the cross. "Reproach hath broken my heart; and I am full of heaviness: and I looked for some to take pity, but there was none; and for comforters, but I found none. They gave me also gall for my meat; and in my thirst they gave me vinegar to drink" (Psalms 69:20-21). The bitter taste of vinegar would confirm that the bitter cup of trembling He first placed to His lips in Gethsemane was now drained. Turning once again to the music of David, which He surely learned as a boy, Jesus died with a Psalm on His lips. "Into thine hand I commit my spirit: thou hast redeemed me, O Lord God of truth" (Psalms 31:5).

There is one more verse I turn to before walking through the flowers and shrubs of the Garden Tomb to contemplate the joy of the resurrection. Isaiah has richer meaning to me after reading the Psalms describing the price of Calvary. "But Zion said, The Lord hath forsaken me, and my Lord hath forgotten me. Can a woman forget her sucking child, that she should not have compassion on the son of her womb? Yea, they may forget, yet will I not forget thee. Behold, I have graven thee upon the palms of my hands" (Isaiah 49:14-16).

When I am tempted to think I have been forgotten or forsaken as did ancient Israel, I turn to these verses. The prints of the nails—nails Isaiah knew would pierce the healing hands of the Messiah—are the Savior's answer to us all. He cannot forget us, for these wounds of His compassion testify that the pain and sorrows of life do not mean that God does not love us. It is to the wounded Christ that we may turn when we feel the shadows of the world closing around us.

There is a natural lightening of the spirit that I feel when I leave Calvary and walk the few yards that bring me to the entrance of the Garden Tomb. I have marked my scriptures that I might be prepared to read them while inside the empty tomb. Did not the angels themselves on the morning of the resurrection invite us all to visit this holy place and contemplate the joy it means for us all? "He is not here: for he is risen, as he said. Come, see the place where the Lord lay" (Matthew 28:6).

The burial chamber in the Garden Tomb. "Wilt thou shew wonders to the dead? shall the dead arise and praise thee? Selah. Shall thy loving kindness be declared in the grave? or thy faithfulness in destruction? Shall thy wonders be known in the dark? and thy righteousness in the land of forgetfulness?" (Psalm 88:10-12). The Doctrine and Covenants answers the psalmist's question: "While this vast multitude waited and conversed, rejoicing in the hour of their deliverance from the chains of death, the Son of God appeared, declaring liberty to the captives who had been faithful; And there he preached to them the everlasting gospel, the doctrine of the resurrection and redemption of mankind from the fall, and from individual sins on conditions of repentance. And so it was made known among . . . the unrighteous as well as the faithful, that redemption had been wrought through the sacrifice of the Son of God upon the cross" (D&C 138:18-19, 35).

WHILE HE LAY IN THE TOMB, His mission in mortality now over, He began His ministry among the dead. There were many in the spirit prison who needed the hope of His triumph. I open my scriptures to Isaiah, who assures us all that Jesus will visit those in prison. "And they shall be gathered together, as prisoners are gathered in the pit, and shall be shut up in the prison, and after many days shall they be visited" (Isaiah 24:22). Not only will He visit them, but Isaiah assures us He will free them. "I have called thee in righteousness . . . . to open the blind eyes, to bring out the prisoners from the prison, and them that sit in darkness out of the prison house" (Isaiah 42:6-7).

I turn now to Job, he who suffered so overwhelmingly, and yet found strength in his Redeemer. "Oh that my words were now written!" he began. "Oh that they were printed in a book! That they were graven with an iron pen and lead in the rock for ever! For I know that my redeemer liveth, and that he shall stand in the latter day upon the earth: And though after my skin worms destroy this body, yet in my flesh shall I see God" (Job 19:23-26).

Here in the semi-darkness of the tomb, the words of Jonah in the belly of the whale strike home. "I cried by reason of mine affliction unto the Lord, and he heard me; out of the belly of hell cried I, and thou heardest my voice . . . I went down to the bottoms of the mountains; the earth with her bars was about me for ever: yet thou hast thou brought up my life from corruption, O Lord my God" (Jonah 2:2, 6). There is no place one can go where the mercy of the Lord cannot reach. He hears our cries from the depths of hell and when we are caught in the prison of the earth. He will free us from both. Jonah's plight, symbolic of the universal condition of death, was certainly not far from Jesus' mind when He declared, "For as Jonas was three days and three nights in the whale's belly; so shall the Son of man be three days and three nights in the heart of the earth" (Matthew 12:40).

I read Hosea's testimony next—written as Christ addresses death itself—assuring us all with his words that death will be overcome; for life, through Christ, is everlasting. "I will ransom them from the power of the grave; I will redeem them from death: O death, I will be thy plagues; O grave, I will be thy destruction" (Hosea 13:14).

Addressing all of us, the Savior promises that His victory is a shared victory in which we all partake. "Thy dead men shall live, together with my dead body shall they arise. Awake and sing, ye that dwell in dust: for thy dew is as the dew of herbs, and the earth shall cast out the dead" (Isaiah 26:19). I cannot help but think as I read Isaiah that Joseph F. Smith, in his vision of Christ's visit in the spirit world, described the waiting righteous as falling on their knees before their Lord and singing to Him out of the full joy of their hearts (D&C 138:23).

I cannot stay longer in the tomb, for there are many who also want to feel the testimony of this place, but I pause for one more shared moment with the prophets of the Old Testament. Ezekiel saw in vision a valley filled with dry bones. "Son of man, can these bones live?" he was asked. There "was a noise," Ezekiel said, "and behold a shaking, and the bones came together, bone to his bone. And when I beheld, lo, the sinews and the flesh came up upon them, and the skin covered them above: . . . and the breath came into them, and they lived, and stood upon their feet . . . . O my people, I will open your graves, and cause you to come up out of your graves, ... And shall put my spirit in you and ye shall live" (Ezekiel 37:3, 7-8,10,12,14).

When I have finished this last day's journey with the Savior, my faith is strengthened and my appreciation for the Atonement is expanded. But I also express gratitude to my Father in Heaven for revealing such deep things of the soul through the beauty of the Old Testament. The poetry of the prophets' words never fails to move me, and I sometimes wonder if they did not know their Savior in an intimate manner which only the foresight of prophetic gifts can bring. I am thankful that they were allowed to share that insight with us all. For that purpose they were called, and the Lord will forever smile upon their labors as He sees how the power of their words continue to inspire and lift.

THE SECOND COMING

(Opposite page) Light breaking through the clouds. "For since the beginning of the world men have not heard, nor perceived by the ear, neither hath the eye seen, O God, beside thee, what he hath prepared for him that waiteth for him" (Isaiah 64:4). Throughout the pages of this sacred text, Isaiah records the anticipatory pleadings of Israel for the return of their King of Kings, or as Haggai called Him, "the desire of all nations" (Haggai 2:7).

The vision of the prophets was not limited to the mortal ministry of the Savior. They also saw the events associated with His second coming, and longed for that day just as we continue to do. Isaiah prayed, "Oh that thou wouldest rend the heavens, that thou wouldest come down, that the mountains might flow down at thy presence" (Isaiah 64:1). He described the Savior as appearing in red as one that "treadeth in the winefat" (Isaiah 63:1-2). He has cleansed the world as He promised.

From the Temple Mount, we can look up the slopes of the Mt. of Olives to the east. One day, the Messiah will come to this mountain, "and his feet shall stand in that day upon the mount of Olives, . . . and [it] shall cleave in the midst thereof . . . and there shall be a very great valley; and half of the mountain shall remove toward the north, and half of it toward the south" (Zechariah 14:4). A wonderful reconciliation will then take place, as the Messiah greets His people. "And I will pour upon the house of David, and upon the inhabitants of Jerusalem, the spirit of grace and of supplications: and they shall look upon me whom they have pierced, and they shall mourn for him, as one mourneth for his only son . . . And one shall say unto him, What are these wounds in thine hands? Then he shall answer, Those with which I was wounded in the house of my friends" (Zechariah 12:10; 13:6).

CREDITS

PHOTOGRAPHS, MAPS, AND ENGRAVINGS

Endsheet: *Terra Sancta* map, 1629.

p. *ii*   En-gedi oasis, © Floyd Holdman.

p. *v*   Olive tree terraces, © Don Thorpe.

p. *vi*   Beersheba grove at sunset, © Don Thorpe.

p. 1   Woman and child in field outside Bethlehem, © Don Thorpe.

p. 2   Moon over Mediterranean Sea, © Don Thorpe.

p. 2   Footprint in sand, © Don Thorpe.

p. 4   Pink clouds at sunset, © Willie Holdman.

p. 5   Bird in tree near Nazareth, © John Telford.

p. 5   Red lilies, © Don Thorpe.

p. 5   *The Sixth Day of Creation,* engraving by Julius Schnorr von Carolsfeld, *Treasury of Bible Illustrations,* Dover Publications.

p. 6   *The Covenant of the Rainbow,* engraving by Julius Schnorr von Carolsfeld, *Treasury of Bible Illustrations,* Dover Publications.

p. 7   Dead Sea waves on shore, © Intellectual Reserve, Inc. Photographer: Wayne Doman. Used by Permission.

p. 8   Rainbow, © Willie Holdman.

p. 9   *The Confusion of Tongues,* engraving by Gustave Doré, *The Doré Bible Illustrations,* Dover Publications.

p. 10   Bedouin children running, © John Telford.

p. 10   Jewish boy, © John Telford.

p. 12   *Rebekah Gives Abraham's Servant Water,* engraving by Julius Schnorr von Carolsfeld, *Treasury of Bible Illustrations,* Dover Publications.

p. 12   Woman at well, © Don Thorpe.

p. 13   Camel caravan in Egypt, © Floyd Holdman.

p. 14   *Jacob and Rachel at the Well,* engraving by Julius Schnorr von Carolsfeld, *Treasury of Bible Illustrations,* Dover Publications.

p. 14   Shepherd with flock, © Don Thorpe.

p. 15   *Jacob's Family Tree,* H. C. Tunison Publisher.

p. 16   Young Arab woman, © Don Thorpe.

p. 17   Bedouin woman at tent, © Don Thorpe.

p. 17   Bedouin tent, © Floyd Holdman.

p. 18   Bedouin family, © Floyd Holdman.

p. 18   Jewish child in alley, © John Telford.

p. 19   Bedouin mother and child, © Floyd Holdman.

p. 20   Temple of Luxor, © Floyd Holdman.

p. 20   Hieroglyphics from the Temple of Karnak, © John Telford.

p. 21   *Joseph Sold by His Brethren,* engraving by Gustave Doré, *The Doré Bible Illustrations,* Dover Publications.

p. 21   Temple of Luxor, © John Telford.

p. 22   *Life and Travels of Abraham,* drawn by Abraham Ortelius (Flemish, 1527-1598).

p. 23   Beersheba ruins, © Intellectual Reserve, Inc. Photographer: Wayne Doman. Used by Permission.

p. 23   Dove on barbed wire, © D. Kelly Ogden.

p. 24   Well at Beersheba, © Intellectual Reserve, Inc. Photographer: Wayne Doman. Used by Permission.

p. 24   *The Sacrifice of Isaac,* © Julius Schnorr von Carolsfeld, *Treasury of Bible Illustrations,* Dover Publications.

p. 25   Dome of the Rock, © Don Thorpe.

p. 26   Pyramid of Chaeops, © Floyd Holdman.

p. 27   *Jacob's Reconciliation with Esau,* engraving by Julius Schnorr von Carolsfeld, *Treasury of Bible Illustrations,* Dover Publications.

p. 27   *Joseph Makes Himself Known to His Brethren,* engraving by Gustave Doré, *The Doré Bible Illustrations,* Dover Publications.

p. 28   Nile at Luxor, © John Telford.

p. 28   Camels and Great Pyramids of Giza, © Floyd Holdman.

p. 29   Man and water buffalo on Nile, © Floyd Holdman.

p. 30   Tomb of Patriarchs at Hebron, © Don Thorpe.

p. 31   *Jacob's Dream,* engraving by Julius Schnorr von Carolsfeld, *Treasury of Bible Illustrations,* Dover Publications.

p. 31   Bethel, © Don Thorpe.

p. 32   Bedouin in Sinai Desert, © Floyd Holdman.

p. 33   Flowering bushes and date palm in Egypt, © John Telford.

p. 34   *The Finding of Moses,* engraving by Gustave Doré, *The Doré Bible Illustrations,* Dover Publications.

p. 34   Sinai Desert, © Don Thorpe.

p. 35   *Map of Exodus,* drawn by Jan Janssonius, 1658.

p. 36   *Moses Striking the Rock in Horeb,* engraving by Gustave Doré, *The Doré Bible Illustrations,* Dover Publications.

p. 36   Sands of the Sinai Desert, © D. Kelly Ogden.

p. 37   *Map of Exodus Trail,* H. C. Tunison Publisher.

p. 38   Crocodile fish, © Linda Nelson.

p. 38   Butterfly fish, © Linda Nelson.